SMASH POP HITS 2002

W9-BCJ-772

PROJECT MANAGER: CAROL CUELLAR
ART DESIGN: KEN REHM

CONTENTS

ALL OR NOTHING

Words and Music by
WAYNE ANTHONY HECTOR
and STEVE MAC

All or Nothing - 6 - 1

I've had the rest of you, now I want the best of you, I don't care if that's_ not fair.__
I've had the rest of you, now I want the best of you. It's time to show_ and tell.__ } 'Cause I want it

Chorus:

all or noth - ing__ at all. There's no - where left__ to__

fall when you reach the bot - tom. It's now or nev - er. Is__ it

all or are we__ just friends? Is this how__ it

me in your life._____ 'Cause I want it all   or noth - ing____ at

all.   There's no - where left____ to____ fall_____   It's now or nev - er.   Is   it

Chorus:

all   or noth - ing____ at all.   There's no - where left____ to____

fall when you reach the bot - tom. It's now   or nev - er.   Is____ it

all or are we just friends? Is this how it

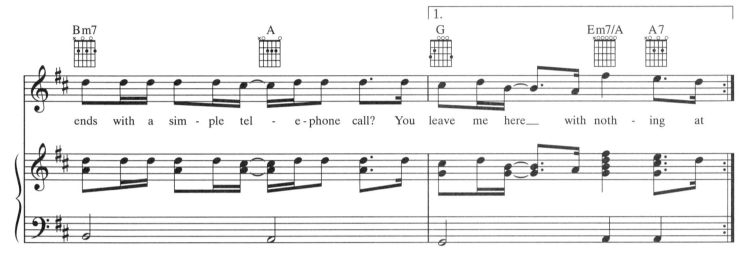

ends with a sim-ple tel-e-phone call? You leave me here with noth-ing at

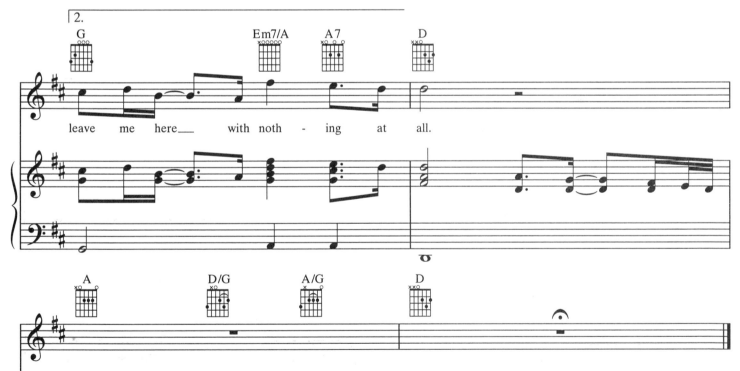

leave me here with noth-ing at all.

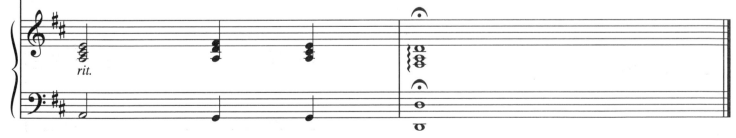

AM TO PM

Moderate dance groove ♩ = 112

Chorus:

Words and Music by
CHRISTINA MILIAN, CHRISTIAN KARLSSON
and PONTUS WINNBERG

(a capella) Some - bod - y hit the lights so we can rock it day and

night. Peo - ple get - tin' down, that's right, from A M to P M.

Ev - 'ry - bod - y look - in' like stars, all the chicks and the fel - las in the

bars. All of ya'll bump - in' this in your cars from A M to P M.

AM to PM - 8 - 1

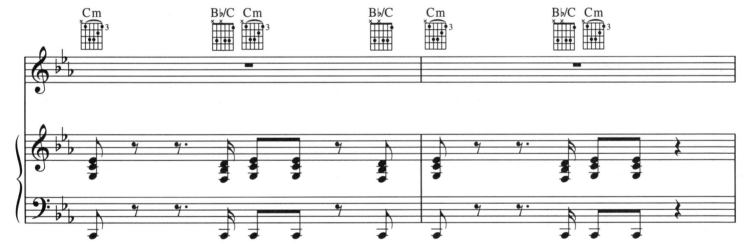

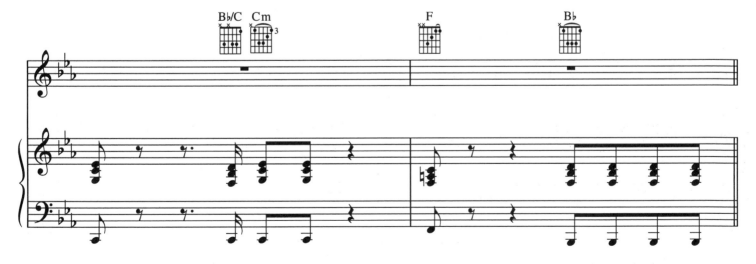

Verse:

1. Ev - 'ry - bod - y wan - na get down_ when you hear the sound_ and you bump the beat_ three
2. *See additional lyrics*

six - ty - five days a year,_ twen - ty - four a day,_ sev - en days a week._ Now, when you're

driv - in' in your four - by - four_ and you turn this up_ on your ster - e - o,_ wheth - er

night or day,_ non - stop you'll play_ and you know you still_ want more._ So,

14

Ev-'ry-bod-y look-in' like stars, all the chicks and the fel-las in the

bars. All of ya'll bump-in' this in your cars from A M to P M.

Oo,_____ yeah, yeah. 2. Ev-'ry-

cars   from A   M to P   M.

From A   M to P   M.

Verse 2:
Ev'rybody in the club, come on,
Keep bobbin' your head now to this song.
You got the beats and breaks and your body shake
And we're doin' it all night long.
Any time or place, any place or time,
No, we don't need no sleep
Three sixty-five days a year, twenty-four a day,
Seven days a week.
(To Pre-chorus:)

ALL FOR YOU

Words and Music by
JANET JACKSON, JAMES HARRIS III,
TERRY LEWIS, WAYNE GARFIELD,
DAVID ROMANI and MAURO MALAVASI

Moderately ♩ = 112

All my girls at the par-ty, look at that bod-y, shak-in' that thing like ya nev-er did see. Got a

nice pack-age al-right. Guess I'm gon-na have to ride__ it to-night. All my

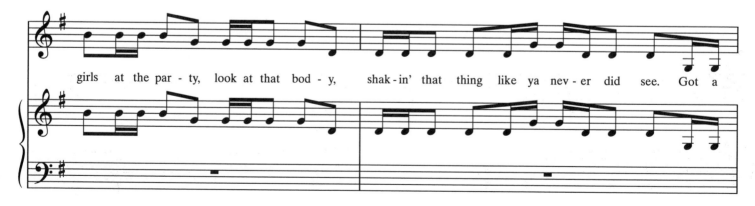

girls at the par-ty, look at that bod-y, shak-in' that thing like ya nev-er did see. Got a

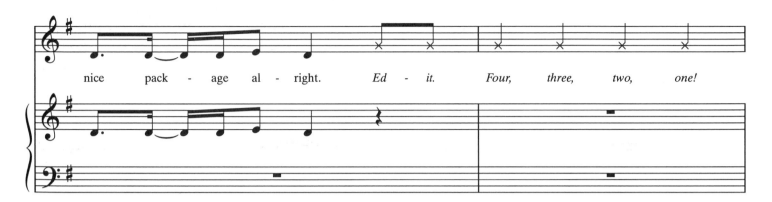

nice pack - age al - right. *Ed - it.* *Four,* *three,* *two,* *one!*

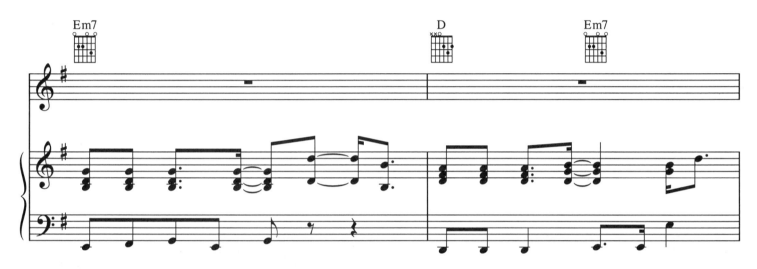

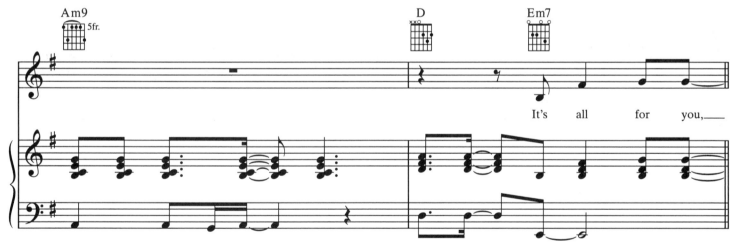

It's all for you,___

Chorus:

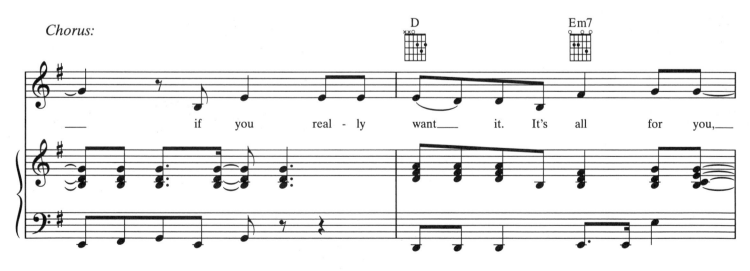

___ if you real - ly want___ it. It's all for you,___

if you say you need__ it. It's all for you,__

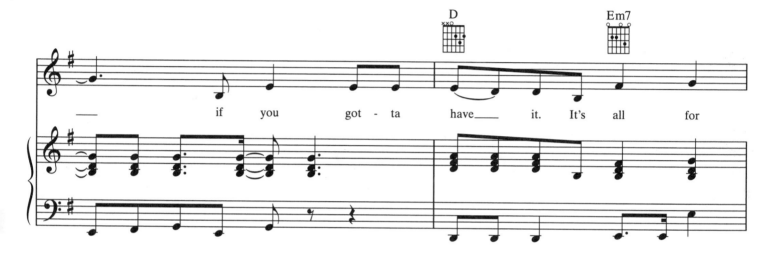

__ if you got-ta have__ it. It's all for

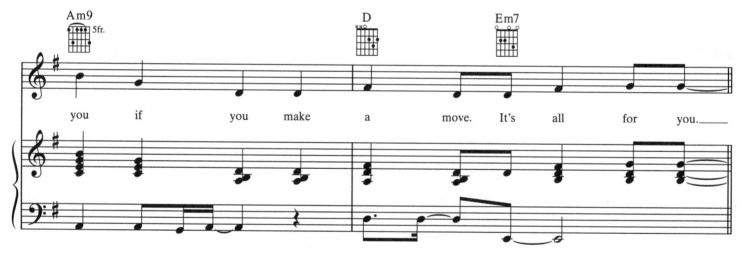

you if you make a move. It's all for you.__

Verse:

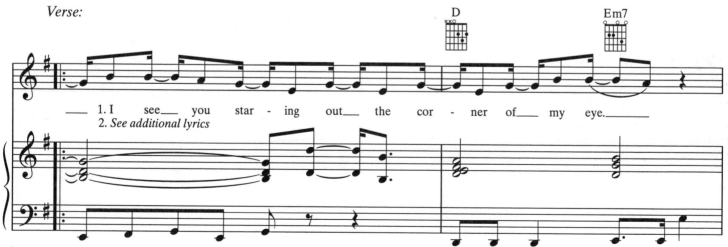

__ 1. I see__ you star-ing out__ the cor-ner of__ my eye.
2. *See additional lyrics*

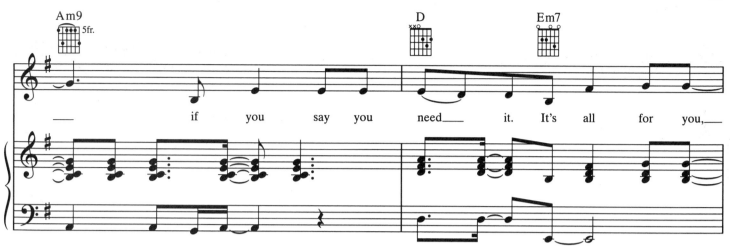

if you say you need___ it. It's all for you,___

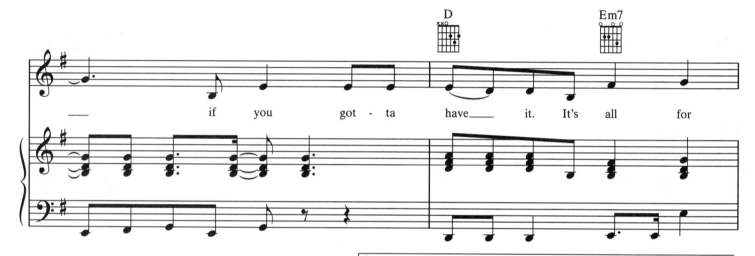

if you got-ta have___ it. It's all for

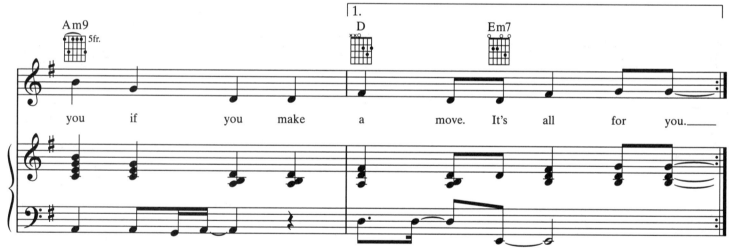

1.

you if you make a move. It's all for you.___

2.

a move. It's all for you.___ Tell me you're the

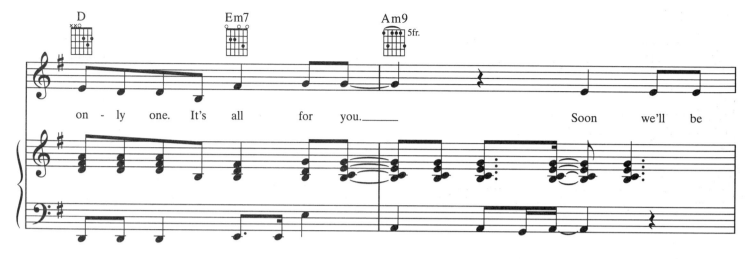

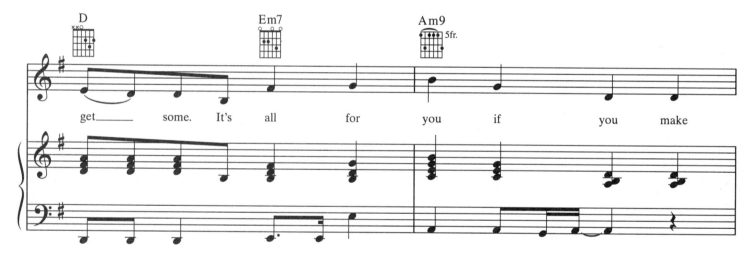

Chorus:

if you real - ly want__ it. It's all for you,____ if you say you
2. Tell me you're the on - ly one. Soon we'll be

need____ it. It's all for you,____ if you gotta
hav - ing fun. Come o - ver here and

Repeat ad lib. and fade

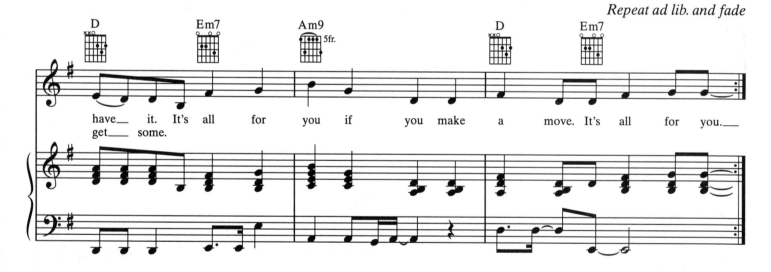

have__ it. It's all for you if you make a move. It's all for you.__
get__ some.

Verse 2:
Can't be afraid or keep me waiting for too long.
Before you know it, I'll be outta here, I'll be gone.
Don't try to be all clever, cute or even shy.
Don't have to work that hard just be yourself,
And let that be your guide.

BECAUSE I GOT HIGH

Words and Music by
AFROMAN

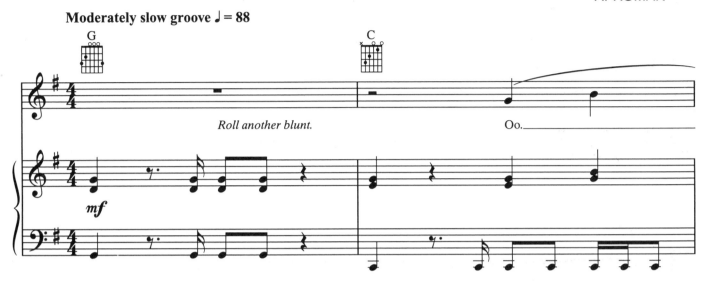

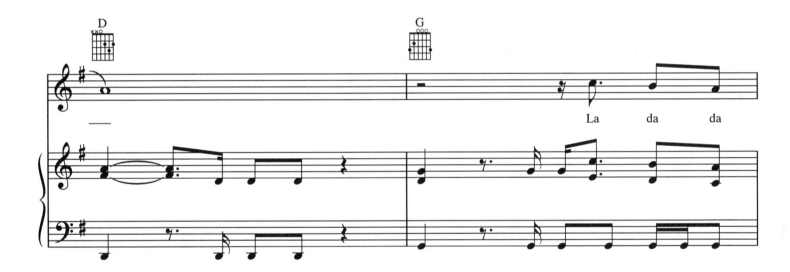

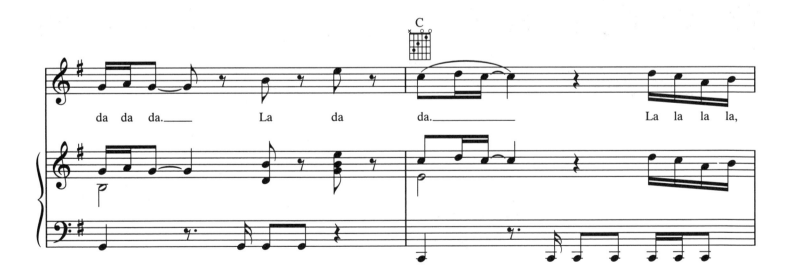

Because I Got High - 3 - 1

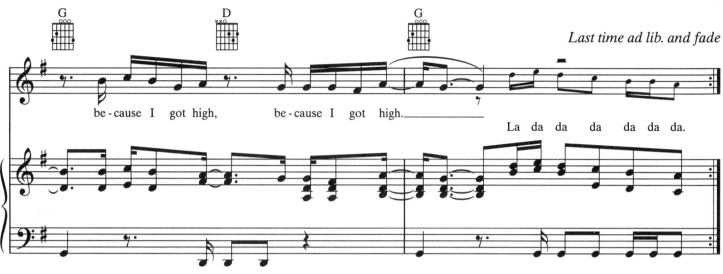

Last time ad lib. and fade

be - cause I got high, be - cause I got high._____ La da da da da da da.

Verse 2:
I was gonna go to class before I got high.
I coulda cheated, and I coulda passed, but I got high.
I'm takin' it next semester, and I know why, yeah;
'Cause I got high, because I got high, because I got high.

Verse 3:
I was gonna go to court before I got high.
I was gonna pay my child support, but then I got high.
They took my whole paycheck, and I know why, yeah;
'Cause I got high, because I got high, because I got high.

Verse 4:
I wasn't gonna run from the cops, but I was high.
I was gonna pull right over and stop, but I was high.
Now I'm a paraplegic, and I know why, yeah;
'Cause I got high, because I got high, because I got high.

Verse 5:
I was gonna make love to you, but then I got high.
I was gonna *** **** *****, too, but then I got high.
Now I'm ******' ***, and I know why, yeah;
'Cause I got high, because I got high, because I got high.

Verse 6:
I messed up my entire life, because I got high.
I lost my kids and wife, because I got high.
Now I'm sleepin' on the sidewalk, and I know why, yeah;
'Cause I got high, because I got high, because I got high.

Verse 7:
I'm-a stop singin' this song, because I'm high.
I'm singin' this whole thing wrong, because I'm high.
And if I don't sell one copy, I'll know why, yeah;
'Cause I'm high, 'cause I'm high, 'cause I'm high.

BABY, COME OVER
(This Is Our Night)

Original Words and Music by
ANDERS BAGGE, ARNTHOR BIRGISSON
and SAMANTHA MUMBA

Chorus:

Baby, Come Over (This Is Our Night) - 6 - 2

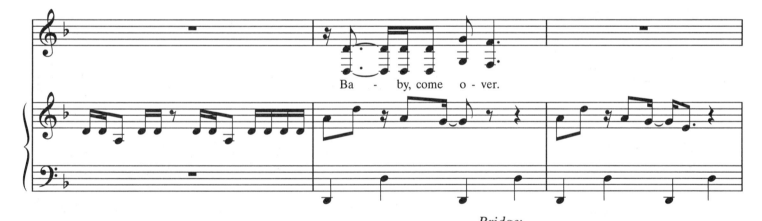

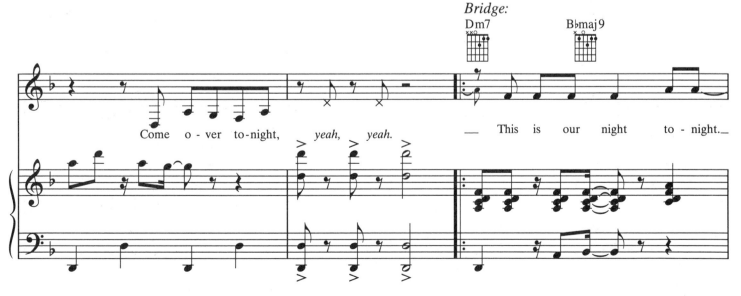

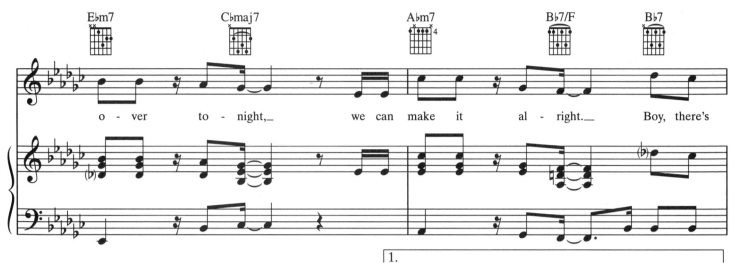

o-ver to-night,_ we can make it al-right._ Boy, there's

no one like you._ Do you feel it too?_____

feel it too?_____

Verse 2:
So when we get together,
If just for a while,
Let's make it happen,
Don't waste any time.
And now I need to find out
What you've all about.
So come over tonight,
Let's sort this out.
(To Chorus:)

BE LIKE THAT

Lryics by
BRAD ARNOLD

Music by
CHRIS HENDERSON and BRAD ARNOLD

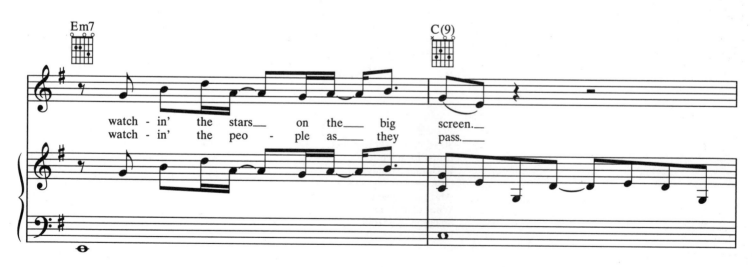

Be Like That - 6 - 1

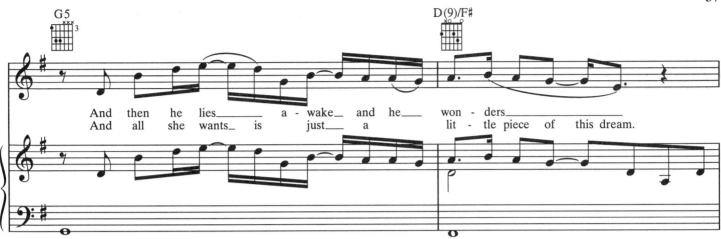

And then he lies_____ a - wake_ and he_____ won - ders_____
And all she wants_ is just_ a lit - tle piece of this dream.

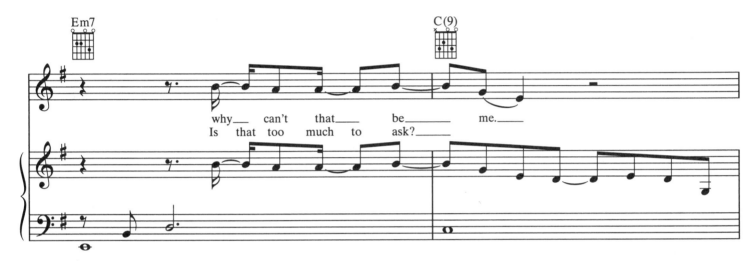

why___ can't that____ be_____ me._____
Is that too much to ask?_____

'Cause in his life,___ he's filled_ with all____ these good_ in - ten - tions.
With a safe__ home,_____ and_ a warm_ bed

He's left a lot___ of things___ he'd rath - er not___ men - tion right now.__
on a qui - et lit - tle street.

Chorus:

BEST I EVER HAD
(GREY SKY MORNING)

Words and Music by
MATTHEW SCANNELL

Gtr. tuned down 1/2 step:
⑥ = E♭ ③ = G♭
⑤ = A♭ ② = B♭
④ = D♭ ① = E♭

Best I Ever Had - 5 - 1

44

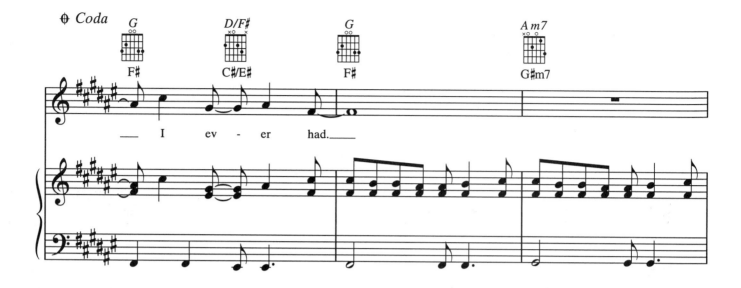

Coda

I ev - er had.____

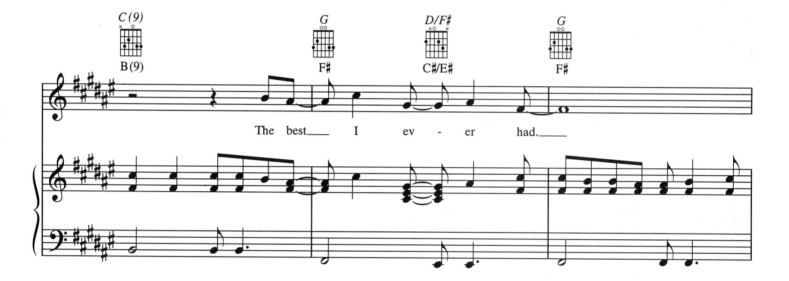

The best__ I ev - er had.____

The best__ I ev - er...____

THE CALL

(Spoken:) "Hello?"
   "Hi, it's me . . . what's up, baby? I'm sorry, listen, I'm gonna be late tonight
     so don't stay up and wait for me, ok?"
   "Where are you?"
   "Say that again . . . you're really dropping out . . . I think my battery must be low . . .
     listen, if you can hear me, we're going to a place nearby, alright? . . . gotta go!"

Words and Music by
MAX MARTIN and RAMI

take it back,__ what's done__ is done.____ One of her friends__ found out__

that she was-n't my on - ly one. And it eats me from__ in - side__

D.S. % al Coda

__ that she's not by__ my side._____ Just be-cause I made that call and lied.

Coda

go!

Lis - ten, ba-by, I'm sor - ry.

Lis-ten, ba-by, I'm sor - ry.

Got-ta

Bridge:

go!"

simile

Verse 3:

3. Let me tell you the sto - ry 'bout the call that changed my des - ti - ny.

Me and my boys__ went out__ just to end up in mis - er - y.

Was a - bout to go home__ when there__ she was__ stand - ing__ in front__ of me.__ I said,

"Hi, I got a lit - tle place near - by. Got - ta

Chorus:

go!" "Lis - ten, ba - by, I'm sor - ry, just wan - na tell you don't wor - ry.

CRAZY

Words and Music by
LINCOLN BROWDER, DARRELL ALLAMBY,
CEDRIC HAILEY and JOEL HAILEY

Verse:

1. Ba - by, I___ a - pol - o - gize___ for all the things___ that I've done,___ that I've done.___
2. *See additional lyrics*

See, I know I've been a fool___ for far too___ long.___ And,

Crazy - 5 - 1

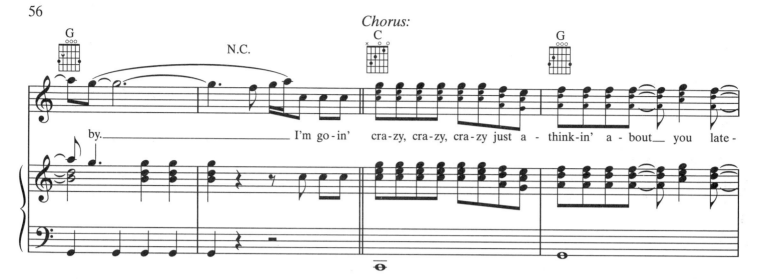

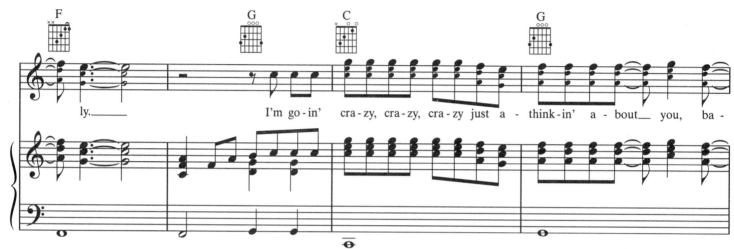

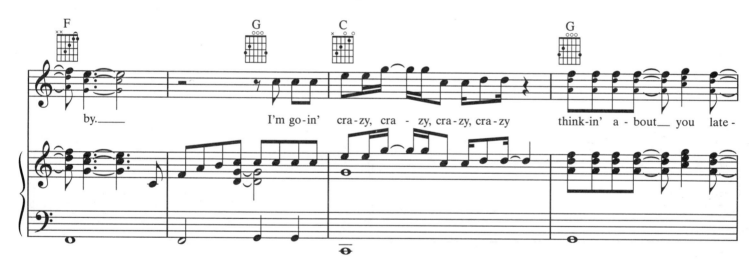

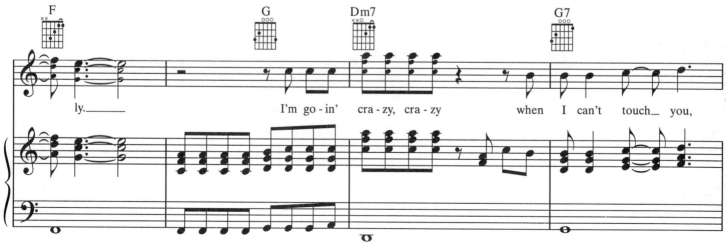

cra-zy, cra-zy   when I can't hold_ you,   cra-zy, cra-zy   when I can't see__ you a-

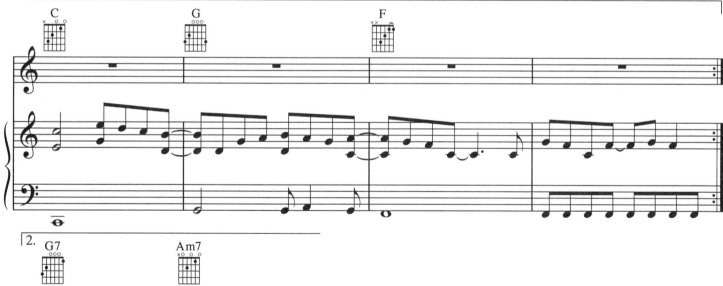

gain._____

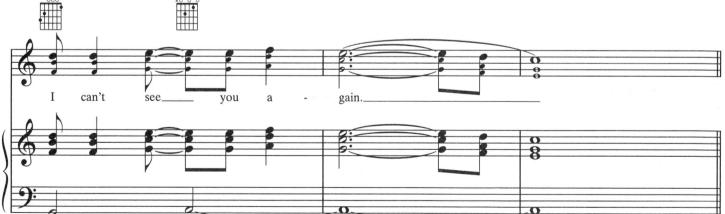

I can't see_____ you a - gain._____

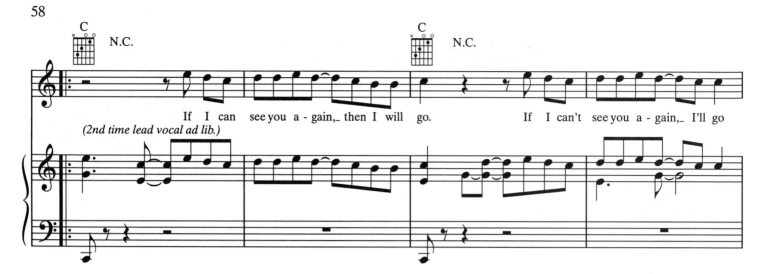

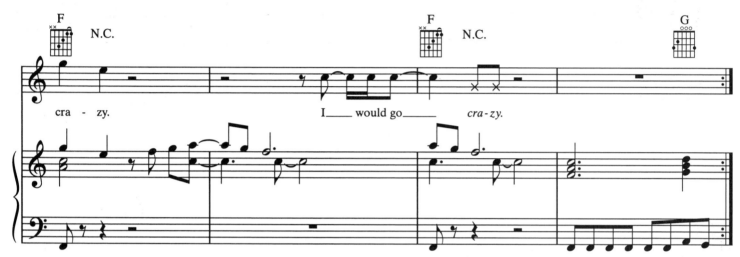

Verse 2:
Now, I finally realize that you are my true love.
And I had a lot of time to think, and you're all I seem to keep thinkin' of, yeah.
And now I know I need ya, each and every day.
I can't live without ya, so don't run away.
Baby, you say that you love me, so why are you leavin' me?
(To Pre-chorus:)

YOU ROCK MY WORLD

Written and Composed by
MICHAEL JACKSON, RODNEY JERKINS,
FRED JERKINS, LaSHAWN DANIELS
and NORA PAYNE

You Rock My World - 5 - 1

Em7 Bm7 Gm7/C Am7/D N.C.

nev-er get e-nough That's_ why I'll al-ways have to have_ you here.

Am7 D Em7 Cmaj9 Bm7

You rocked my world, you know you did._ And ev-'ry-thing I own, I give._ The rar-est

Repeat ad lib. and fade

Am7 D Em7 Cmaj9 Bm7

love, who'd think I'd find__ some-one__ like you__ to call__ mine? You rocked my

Verse 2:
In time, I knew that love would bring
Such happiness to me.
I tried to keep my sanity.
I've waited patiently.
Girl, you know it seems
My life is so complete.
A love that's true because of you.
Keep doing what you do.
Think that I found the perfect love
I've searched for all my life.
(Searched for all my life.)
Think I'd find such a perfect love
That's awesomely so right, girl.
(To Chorus:)

DON'T LET ME BE THE LAST TO KNOW

Words and Music by
R.J. LANGE, SHANIA TWAIN
and KEITH SCOTT

Don't Let Me Be the Last to Know - 6 - 1

Verses 2 & 3:

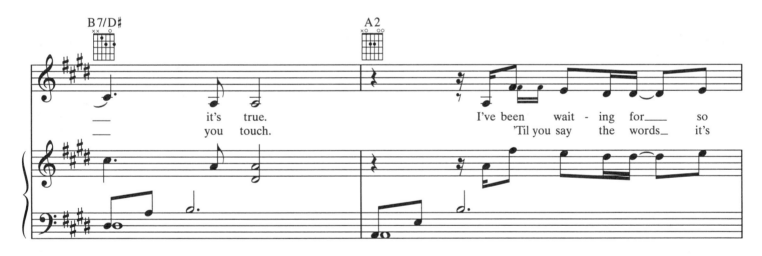

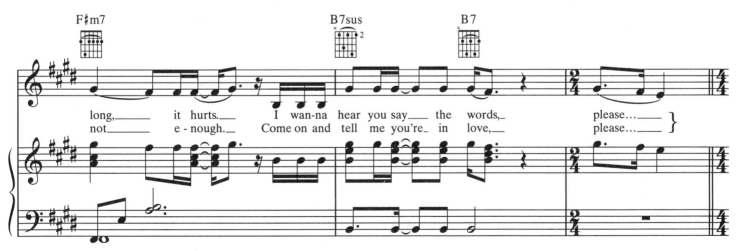

Chorus:

Don't, don't let me be the last to know.— Don't—

— hold— back,— just let it go.— I need—

— to hear— you say— you need— me all— the way.— Oh,

1.

if you love— me so, don't—— let me be the last to know.—

Chorus:

Don't, don't let me be the last to know.___ Don't___

___ hold___ back,___ just let it go.___ I need___

___ to hear___ you say___ you need___ me all___ the way.___ *So, ba-by, if you love me,*

don't___ let me be the last to know._____

DON'T NEED YOU TO
(Tell Me I'm Pretty)

Words and Music by
DIANE WARREN

Moderately slow ♩ = 86

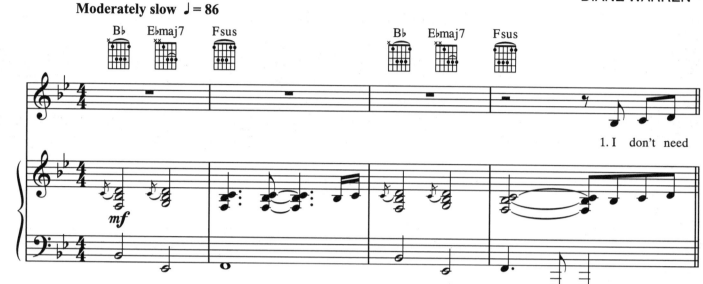

1. I don't need

Verse:

you to tell me I'm pret-ty to make me feel
you to be - lieve in me to make me know I'm worth be -

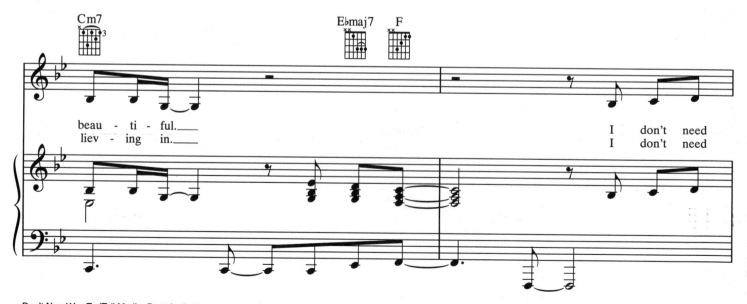

beau - ti - ful.___
liev - ing in.___

I don't need
I don't need

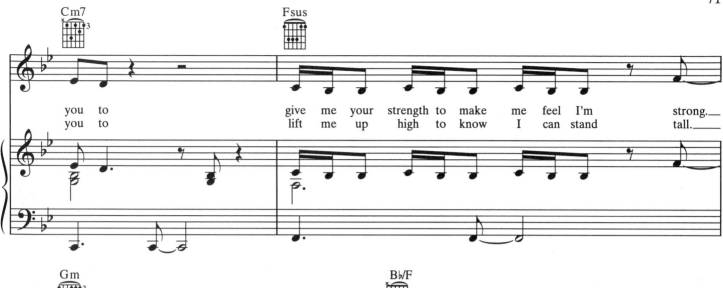

you to

give me your strength to make me feel I'm strong.___

you to

lift me up high to know I can stand tall.___

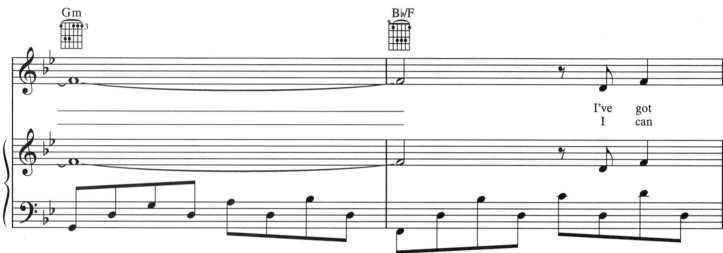

I've got

I can

all of the strength that I need here in-side my own two hands.___

stand my own ground, I can stand proud up-on my own two feet.___

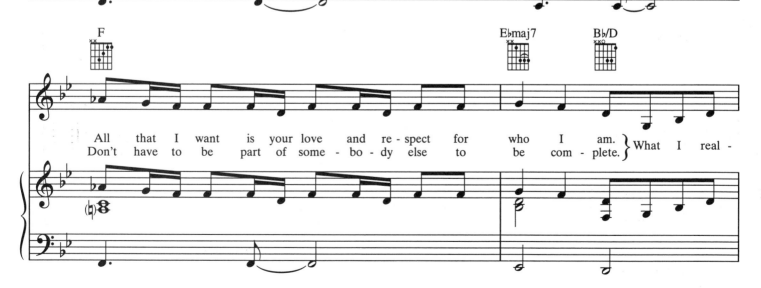

All that I want is your love and re-spect for who I am. } What I real -

Don't have to be part of some-bo-dy else to be com-plete. }

72

Chorus:

Don't Need You To (Tell Me I'm Pretty) - 6 - 6

DROWNING

Words and Music by
RAMI, ANDREAS CARLSSON
and LINDA THOMPSON

1. Don't pre-tend__ you're sor - ry,_____ I know you're not.
2. May - be I'm__ a drift - er,_____ may - be not.

You know you've got__ the pow - er to make me weak__ in - side.__
'Cause I have known__ the safe - ty of float-ing free - ly in__ your arms.__

Drowning - 6 - 1

and my heart beats__ a-gain.__ Ba-by, I can't help__

__ it, you keep me drown-ing in__ your love.__ And ev-'ry-time I try to rise__ a-bove,__

__ I'm swept a-way__ by__ love.__ Ba-by, I can't help__

1.

__ it, you keep me drown-ing in__ your love.__

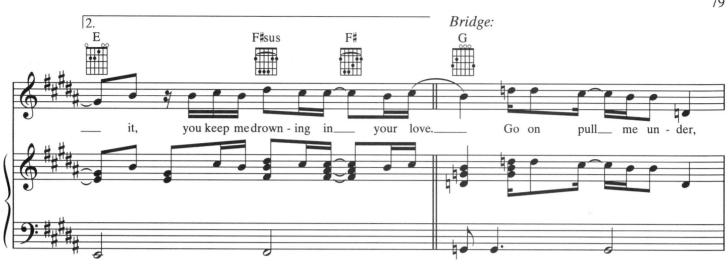

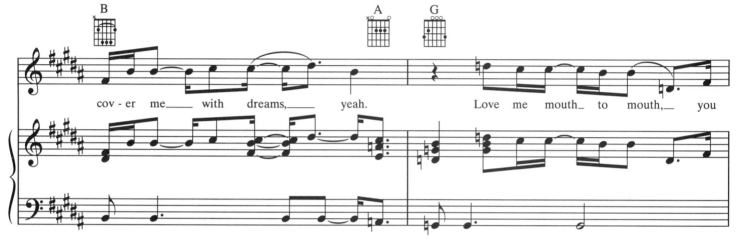

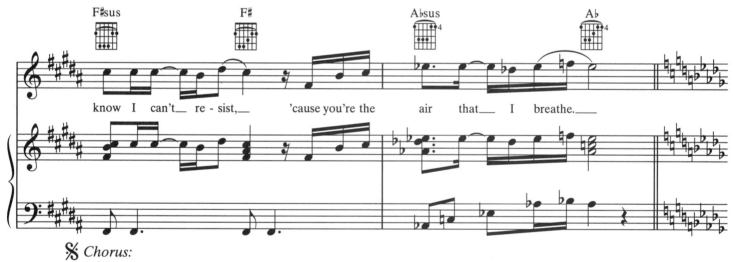

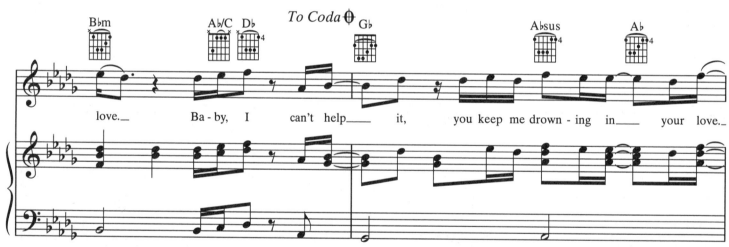

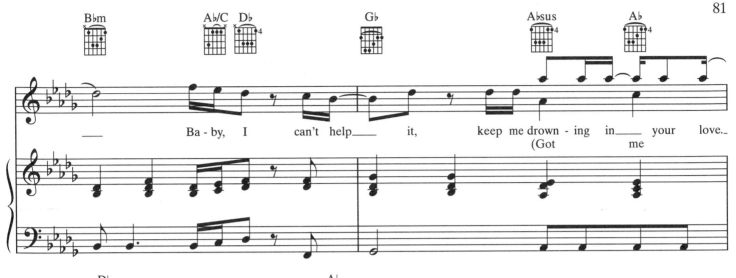

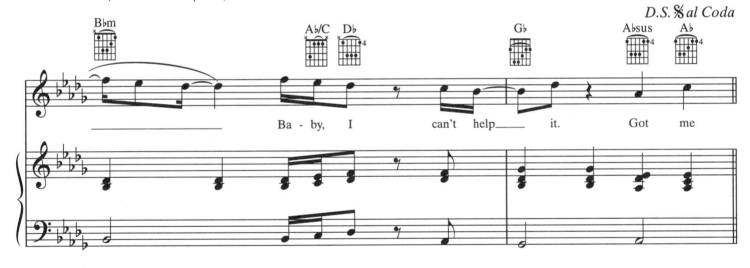

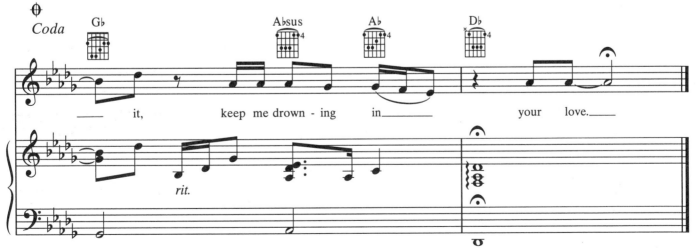

EL ÚLTIMO ADIÓS/THE LAST GOODBYE

Words and Music by
EMILIO ESTEFAN, JR. and GIAN MARCO ZIGNAGO
English Lyrics by JON SECADA and EMILIO ESTEFAN, JR.

1. Se que-bró la cal - ma   y el si - len-cio en rui - do se vol - vió.
2. Na - die va a cam-biar - nos,   na - die nos va a ha-cer per - der la fé.

Que-da-ron des-nu - dos   nues-tra i - ma - gen y   nues-tro do - lor.
Na-die va a ca - llar - nos,   nues-tra fuer - za vuel - ve a re - na - cer.

El Último Adiós/The Last Goodbye - 9 - 1

El Último Adiós/The Last Goodbye - 9 - 2

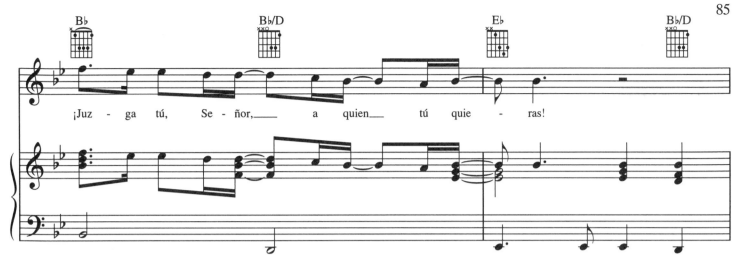

¡Juz - ga tú, Se - ñor,_____ a quien____ tú quie - ras!

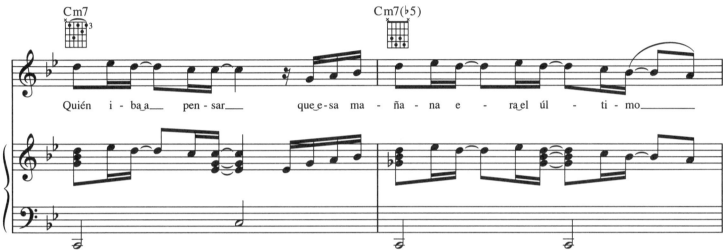

Quién i - ba_a_____ pen - sar_____ que_e-sa ma - ña - na e - ra_el úl - ti - mo_____

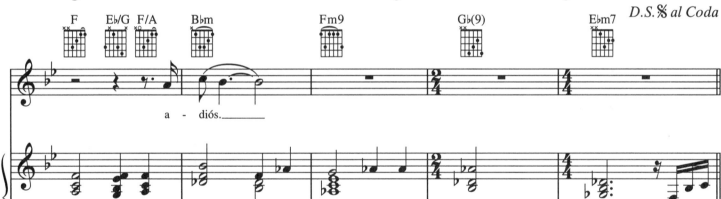

D.S. 𝄋 al Coda

a - diós._____

Coda

¡Di - me si_el_____ do - lor_____ des - pier - ta_al

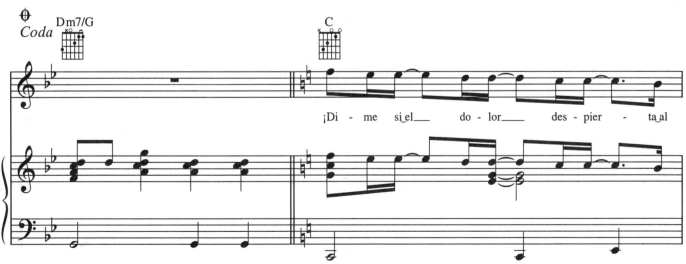

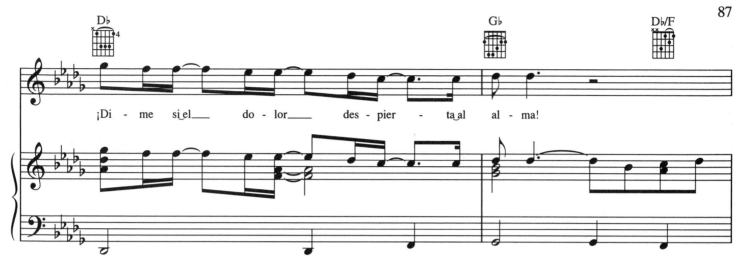

¡Di - me si_el___ do - lor___ des - pier - ta_al al - ma!

¡Di - me si_es___ ca - paz___ de des - per - tar el co - ra - zón!

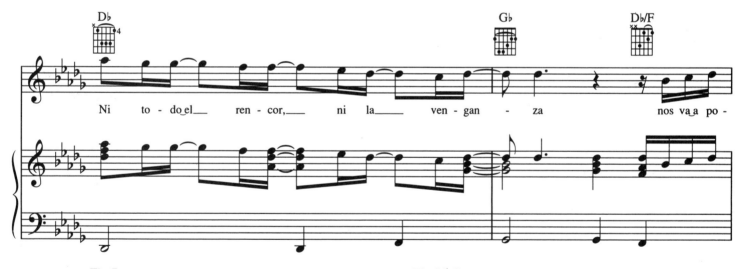

Ni to - do_el___ ren - cor,___ ni la___ ven - gan - za nos va_a po -

der cal - mar___ las ga - nas de ver de nue - vo_a - que - llas ca - ras.

El Último Adiós/The Last Goodbye - 9 - 6

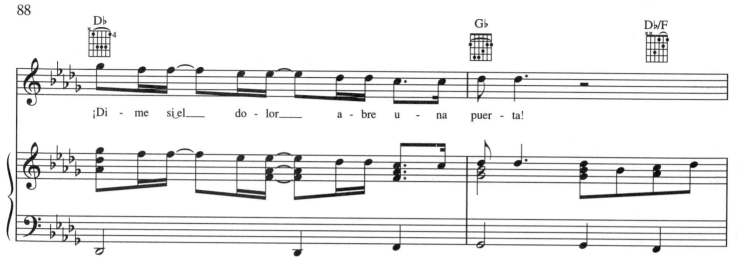

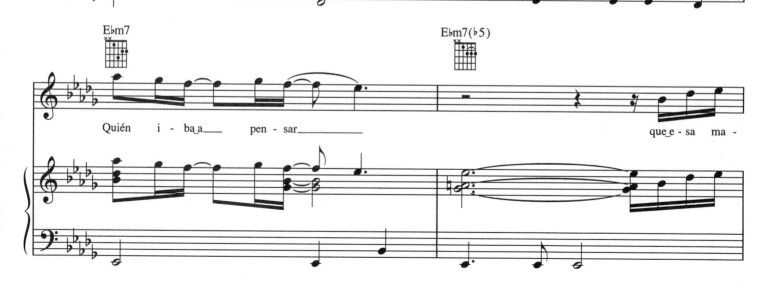

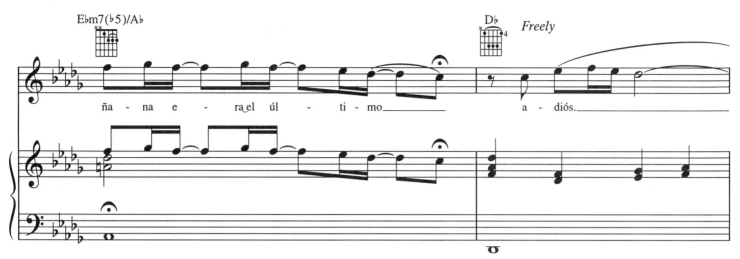

ña - na e - ra_el úl - ti - mo_____ a - diós._____

EL ÚLTIMO ADIÓS/THE LAST GOODBYE

Words and Music by
EMILIO ESTEFAN, JR. and GIAN MARCO ZIGNAGO
English Lyrics by JON SECADA and EMILIO ESTEFAN, JR.

English Translation

It's a different silence,
Things are not the same way anymore.
My eyes could not believe it
When the sky came tumbling down to the floor.
There's so many feelings,
So many fears
We haven't felt before.
Tell me what went wrong
Tell me where's the love.

It's so hard to have this pain without an answer.
How do we begin
To heal so many broken hearts.
How do we begin
To turn the anger.
How do we face the morning after
Without the faces that won't come home again.
Faith is the only thing we've got to hold on.
Love's the only reason that I know we can go on.
No one's gonna change what we believe in.
Who would've ever realized that morning was the last goodbye.

Freedom makes us stronger.
The stars and stripes will never be the same.
Step by step we'll make it,
It's our pride that they can't take away.
One and all together
See the dawn of a brand new day.
America, united we will find a way.

All proceeds donated to The American Red Cross and The United Way.

EVERYWHERE

Words and Music by
MICHELLE BRANCH
and JOHN SHANKS

Everywhere - 9 - 1

Verse 3:

Bridge:

Chorus:

ev - 'ry - where to me.___ { And when I close___ my eyes,___ / And when I catch___ my breath,___ }

___ it's you I see. / ___ it's you I breathe. } You're ev - 'ry - thing___ I know___

___ that makes me be - lieve___ I'm not___ a - lone.___

1.

'Cause you're

Verse 2:
Just tell me how I got this far.
Just tell me why you're here and who you are.
'Cause every time I look, you're never there.
And every time I sleep, you're always there.
(To Chorus:)

FAMILY AFFAIR

Words and Music by
MARY J. BLIGE, ANDRE YOUNG, BRUCE MILLER,
CHYNNAH LODGE, ASIAH LEWIS, CAMARA KAMBON,
MIKE ELIZONDO and MELVIN BRADFORD

Chorus:

Let's get it crunk up-on, have fun up-on, up in this danc-er-y. We got y'all o-pen now, ya float-in' so ya gots to dance for me. Don't need no hat-er-a-tion,

Family Affair - 6 - 1

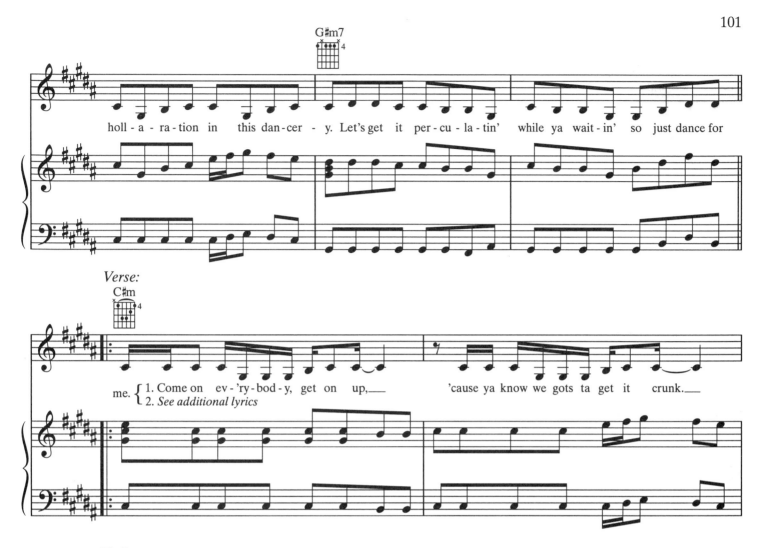

Verse:

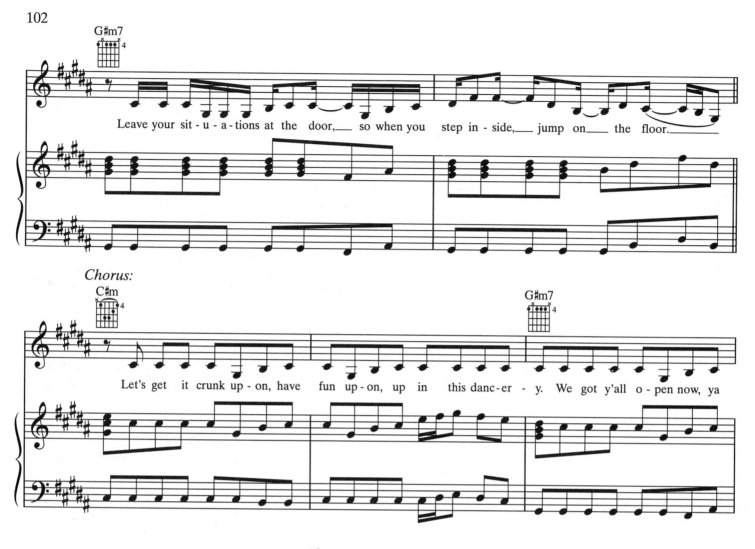

Leave your sit - u - a - tions at the door,___ so when you step in - side,___ jump on___ the floor.___

Chorus:

Let's get it crunk up - on, have fun up - on, up in this danc - er - y. We got y'all o - pen now, ya

float - in' so ya gots to dance for me. Don't need no hat - er - a - tion, holl - a - ra - tion in this dan - cer -

1.

y. Let's get it per - cu - la - tin' while ya wait - in' so just dance for

2.

while ya wait - in' so just dance for

fun to - night, no fights. Turn that Dre track way up high. Mak - in' ya

dance all night and I got some real heat for ya this time. It does - n't

mat - ter if you're white or black. Let's get crunk, 'cause Mar - y's back.

Chorus:

Let's get it crunk up - on, have fun up - on, up in this danc - er -

y. We got y'all o - pen now, ya float - in' so ya gots to dance for

me. Don't need no hat - er - a - tion, holl - a - ra - tion in this dan - cer -

Repeat ad lib. and fade

y. Let's get it per - cu - la - tin' while ya wait - in' so just dance for

Verse 2:
It's only going to be about a matter of time
Before ya get loose and start to lose your mind.
Cop you a drink, go ahead and rock ya ice,
'Cause we're celebrating no more drama in our life.
With the Dre track pumpin', everybody's jumpin'.
Go ahead and twist ya back and get body bumpin'.
I told ya, leave your situations at the door,
So grab somebody and get your ass on the dance floor.
(To Chorus:)

FILL ME IN

Words and Music by
MARK HILL and CRAIG DAVID

Fill Me In - 7 - 1

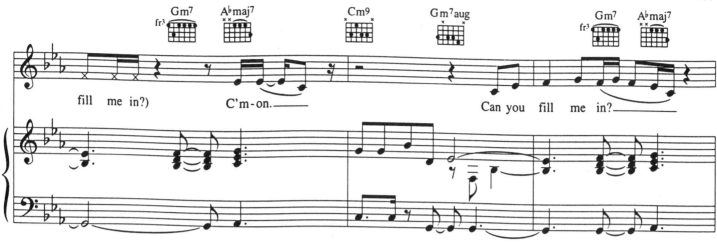

fill me in?)   C'm-on.   Can you fill me in?

(What-cha want,   what-cha want me to do ba - by?)

Can you fill me in?

(Let's talk a - bout it.)

Fill Me In - 7 - 2

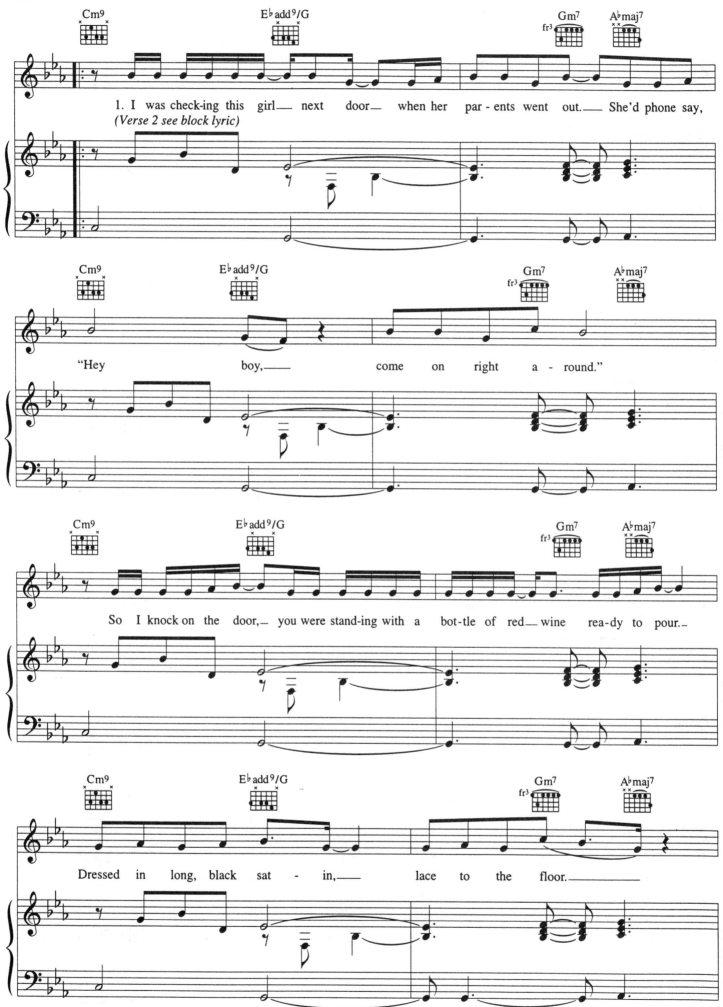

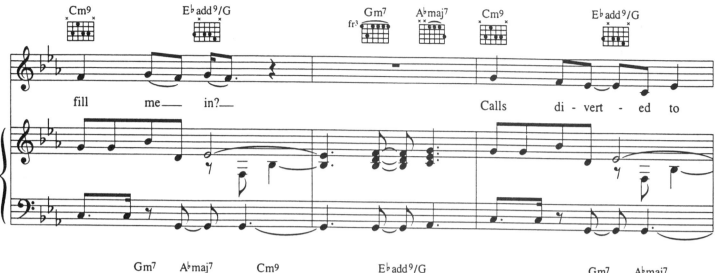

fill me in? Calls di-vert-ed to

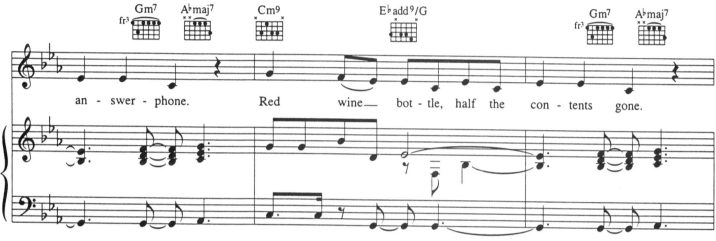

an-swer-phone. Red wine bot-tle, half the con-tents gone.

To Coda ⊕

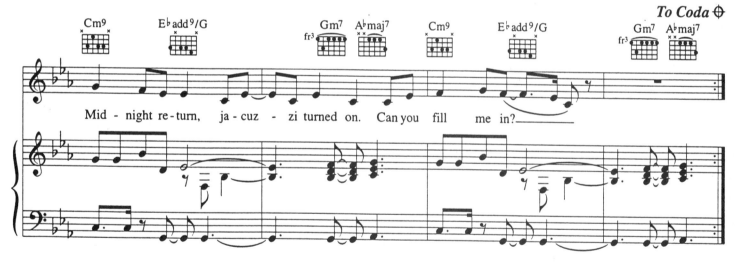

Mid-night re-turn, ja-cuz-zi turned on. Can you fill me in?

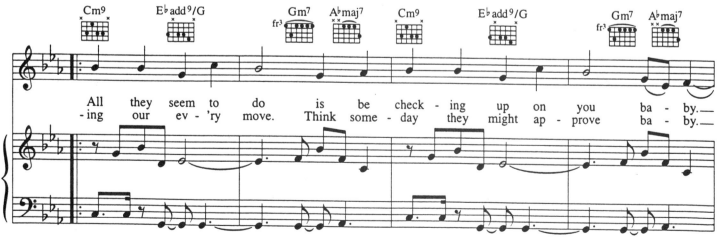

-ing our ev-'ry move. Think some-day they might ap-prove ba-by.

All they seem to do is be check-ing up on you ba-by.

Watch -

Verse 2:

Whenever the coast was clear and she'd ask me to come out
I'd say "Hey girl, come on right around"
So she knocked at the door
I was standing with the keys in my hand to the four-by-four
Jumped in my ride checking that nobody saw
The club we went in, we got down
Bounce, bounce to the rhythm
Saw it was early morning
Thought we'd better be leaving
So I gave you my jacket for you to hold
Told you to wear it cos you felt cold
I mean me and her didn't mean to break the rules
I wasn't trying to play your mum and dad for fools
We were just doing things young people in love do
Parents trying to find out what we were up to.

Saying why can't you keep your promises no more
Saying you'll be home by twelve, come strolling in at four
Out with your girls, but leaving with the boy next door
Can you fill me in? (fill me in)
Wearing a jacket who's property
Said you'd been queuing for a taxi
But you left all your money on the TV (you tell 'em, babe)
Can you fill me in? (can you fill me in).

FOLLOW ME

Words and Music by
MATTHEW SHAFER and
MICHAEL BRADFORD

Moderately ♩ = 112

N.C.

(Vocal a cappella 1st Verse & 1st Chorus) 1. You

Verse:

(3.) don't know how you met me. You don't___ know___ why.___ You can't___
2. *See additional lyrics*

___ turn a-round___ and say___ good-bye.___ All you know___

Follow Me - 5 - 1

want to leave,_____ I can guar - an - tee_____ you won't_____

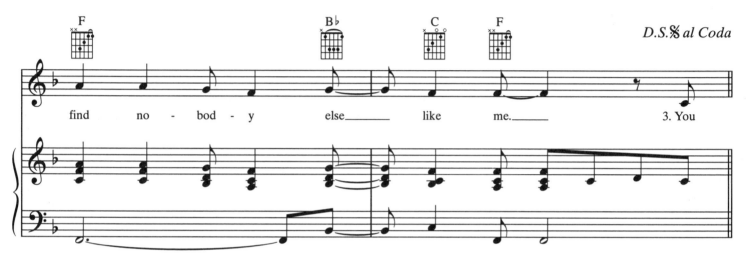

D.S.% al Coda

find no - bod - y else_____ like me._____ 3. You

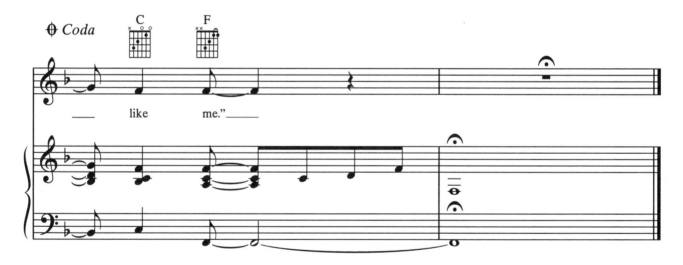

⊕ *Coda*

_____ like me."_____

Verse 2:
I'm not worried 'bout the ring you wear,
'Cause as long as no one knows, then nobody can care.
You're feelin' guilty and I'm well aware,
But you don't look ashamed and, baby, I'm not scared.
(To Chorus:)

FREE

Words and Music by
MYA HARRISON, JAMES HARRIS III, TERRY LEWIS,
ALEXANDER RICHBOURG and TONY TOLBERT

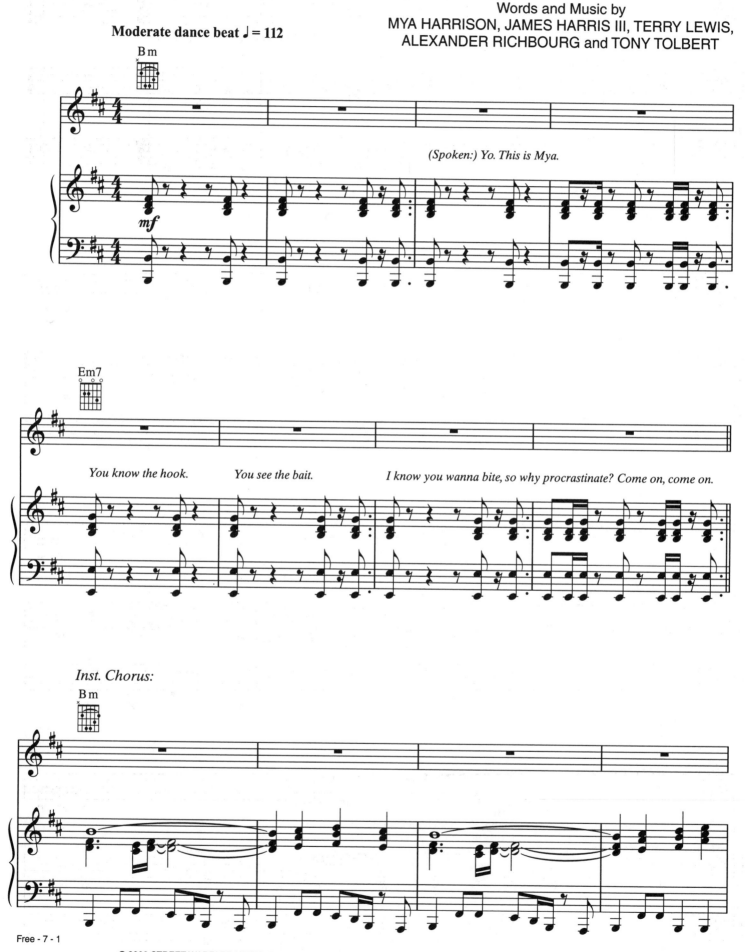

Free - 7 - 1

luck-y, 'cause I feel free to-night. Are you a - vail - a-ble? Did you come

Repeat ad lib. and fade

here a - lone?_____ Won't you hang out with me? I'll freak you on the___ dance___ floor.___

Verse 2:
Now, I don't need a man in my life
Tryin' to tie me down.
And I don't wanna playa
Who got kids all over town.
Don't want his curl juice drippin'
All over my Mercedes seat.
I can't stand a man who thinks
He looks better than me.

Verse 3:
I'm lookin' for a brother who
Likes to have fun.
A fly gentleman who knows
How to please a woman.
Last thing I need is a man that's soft.
He better get it on up and break me off.
Some o' that fly high rise, 6' 5", ain't shy,
And that's the kinda man I need.
Because I'm...
(To Chorus:)

GONE

Words and Music by
JUSTIN TIMBERLAKE and
WADE J. ROBSON

Moderately ♩ = 56

Verse:

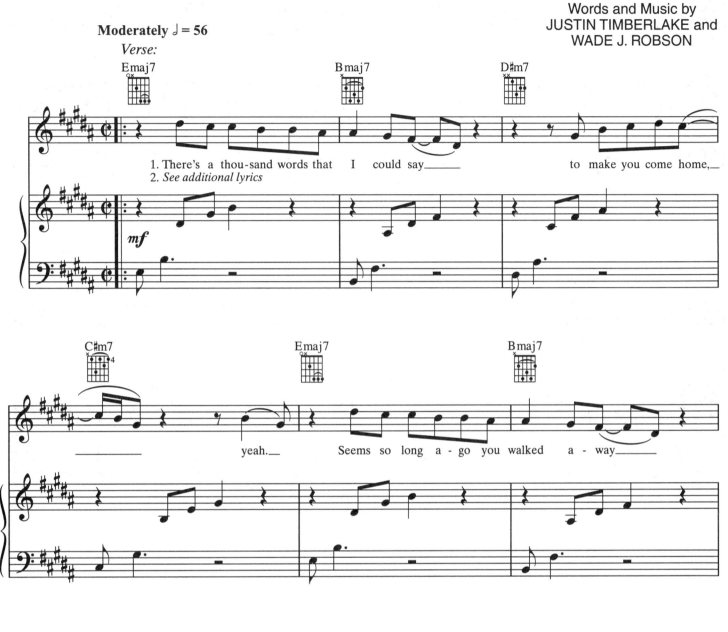

1. There's a thou-sand words that I could say to make you come home,
2. See additional lyrics

yeah. Seems so long a-go you walked a-way

and left me a-lone. And I re-mem-ber what you

Gone - 7 - 1

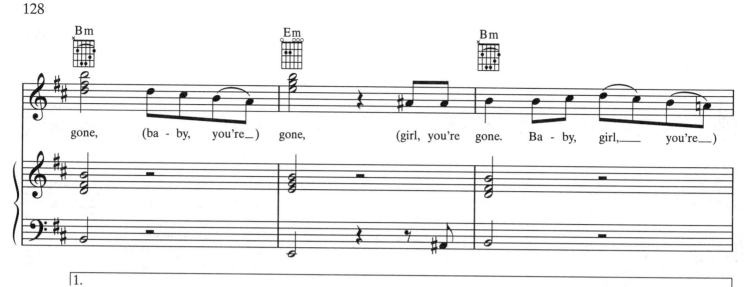

gone, (ba - by, you're__) gone, (girl, you're gone. Ba - by, girl,___ you're__)

1.

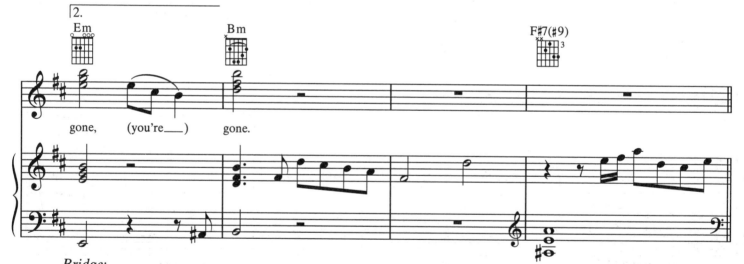

gone, (you're__) gone. (You're...___)

2.

gone, (you're__) gone.

Bridge:

What will I do if I can't be with

you? Tell me, where will I turn to? Ba - by,

who will I be? Now that we are a -

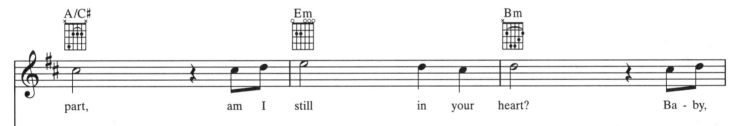

part, am I still in your heart? Ba - by,

why don't you see that I need you here___ with me?___

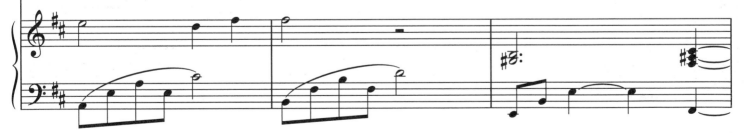

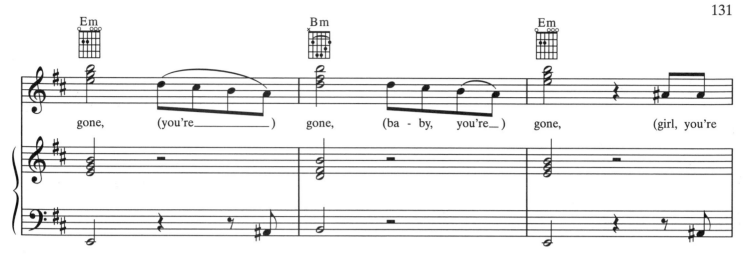

Verse 2:
Now, I don't wanna make excuses, baby.
Won't change the fact that you're gone.
But if there's something that I could do,
Won't you please let me know?
The time is passing so slowly now,
Guess that's my life without you.
And maybe I could change my everyday,
But, baby, I don't want to.
So I'll just hang around and find some things to do
To take my mind off missing you.
And I know in my heart,
You can't say that you don't love me too.
Please say you do, yeah.
(To Chorus:)

GET OVER YOURSELF

Words and Music by
MICHELE VICE-MASLIN,
MATTHEW GERRARD and JOHN KELLER

1. Yeah, I was right there, like the "lit-tle wife." I was ev-'ry-thing that you need, al-ways in line. I was
2. *See additional lyrics*

liv-ing you, lov-ing you, fill-ing your de-si-res. But that was then, this is now, look me in the eyes. And

Get Over Yourself - 6 - 1

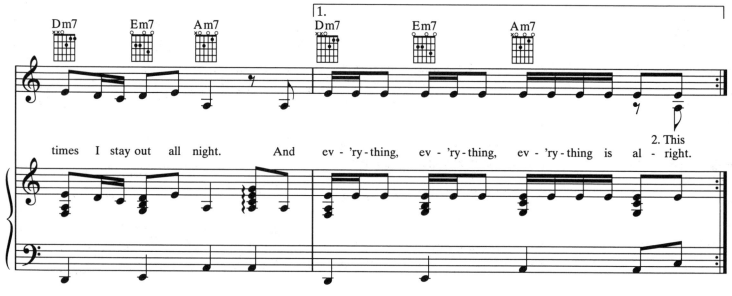

times I stay out all night. And ev-'ry-thing, ev-'ry-thing, ev-'ry-thing is al-right.

2. This

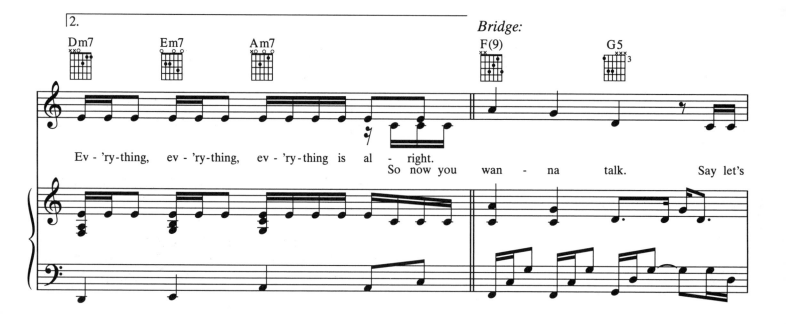

Ev-'ry-thing, ev-'ry-thing, ev-'ry-thing is al-right. So now you wan-na talk. Say let's

do it just once more for luck. Like old times, make up.

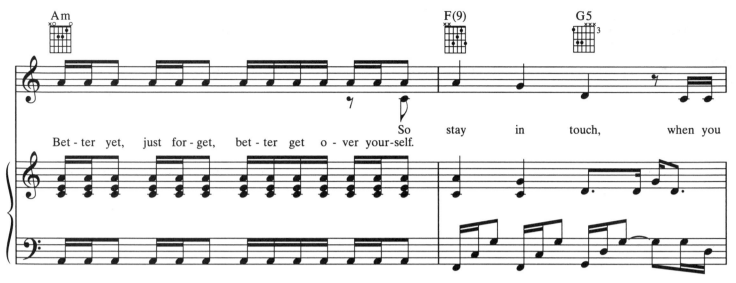

So stay in touch, when you

Bet-ter yet, just for-get, bet-ter get o-ver your-self.

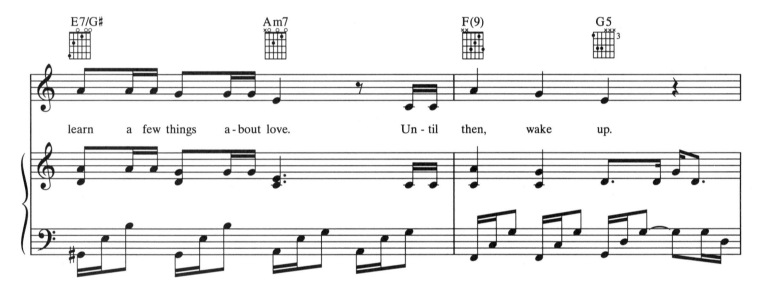

learn a few things a-bout love. Un-til then, wake up.

Chorus:

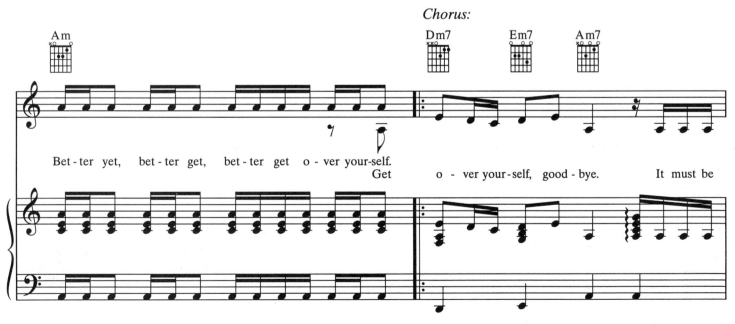

Bet-ter yet, bet-ter get, bet-ter get o-ver your-self.

Get o-ver your-self, good-bye. It must be

hard to be you, yeah, liv-ing in your life. I was al-ways the one to cry. Now,

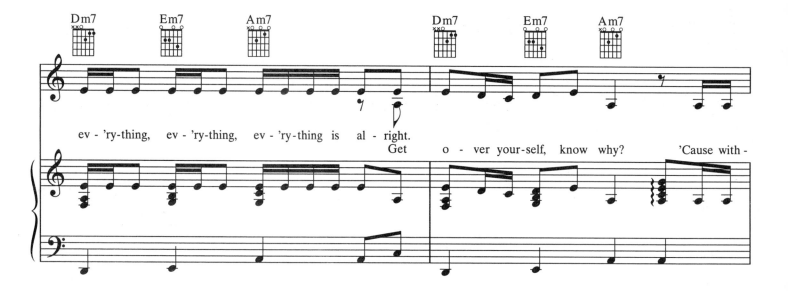

ev-'ry-thing, ev-'ry-thing, ev-'ry-thing is al-right. Get o-ver your-self, know why? 'Cause with-

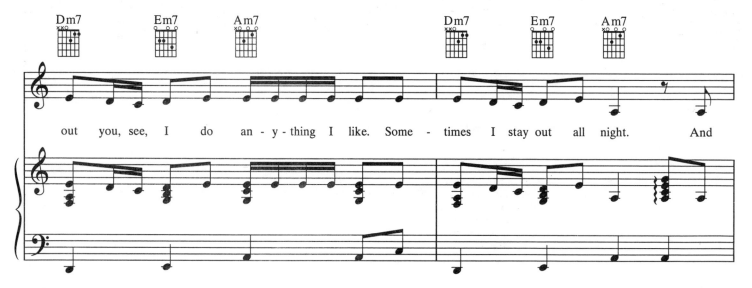

out you, see, I do an-y-thing I like. Some-times I stay out all night. And

Verse 2:
This just can't be it, I keep telling myself.
And every magazine said was me was on the shelf.
I was giving out, giving in, giving way my dreams.
While you put it in, put me down, now I found my self-esteem.
And oh, you won't get me back.
Oh, think I overreact? Well...
(To Chorus:)

HERO

Words and Music by
ENRIQUE IGLESIAS, PAUL BARRY
and MARK TAYLOR

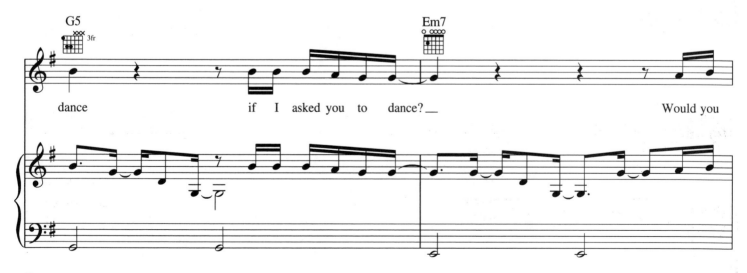

Hero - 7 - 1

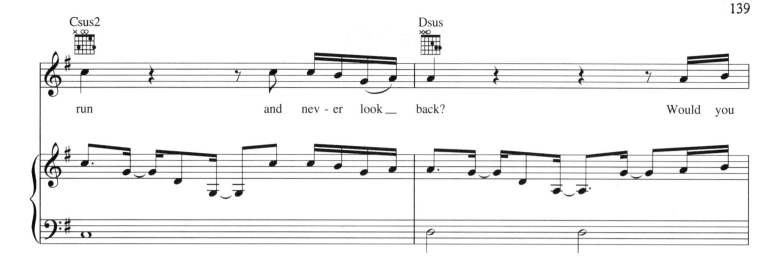

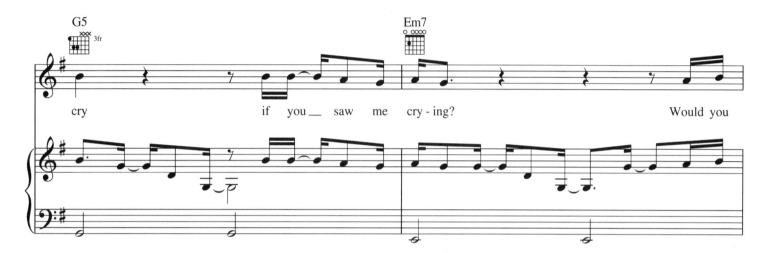

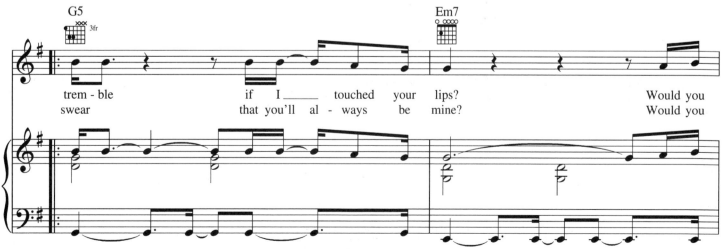

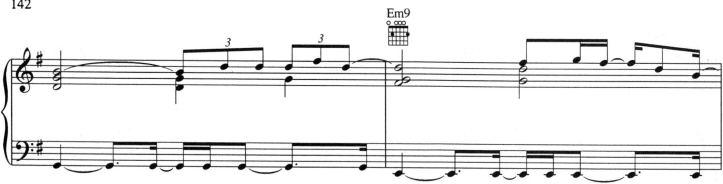

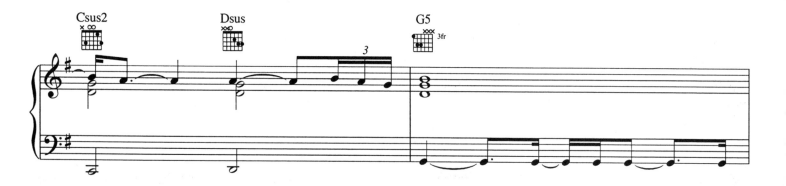

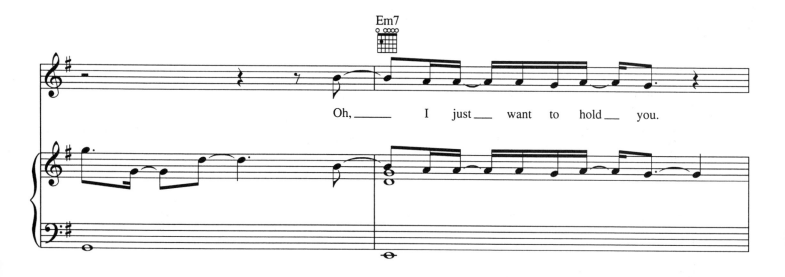

Oh, _____ I just ___ want to hold ___ you.

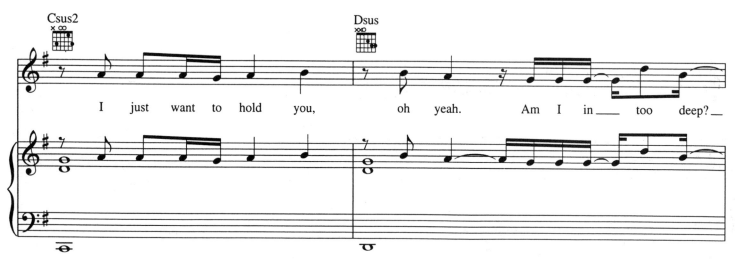

I just want to hold you, oh yeah. Am I in ___ too deep? ___

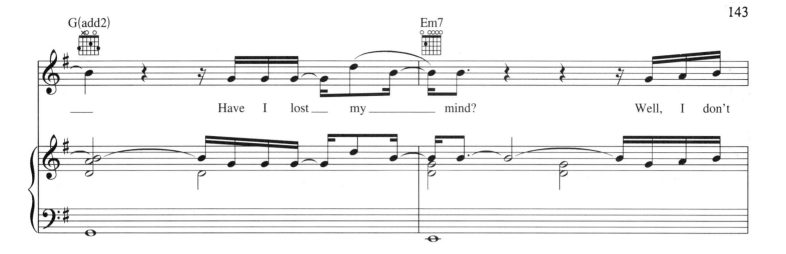

Have I lost ___ my _____ mind? Well, I don't

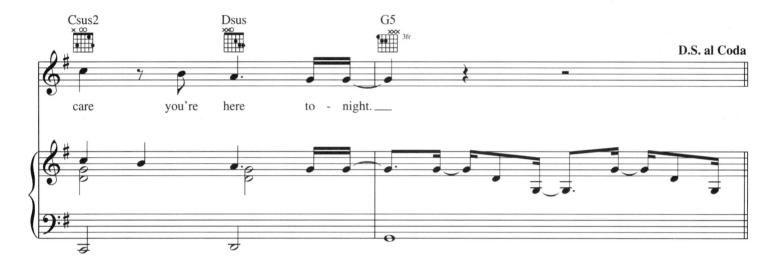

care you're here to - night. ___

D.S. al Coda

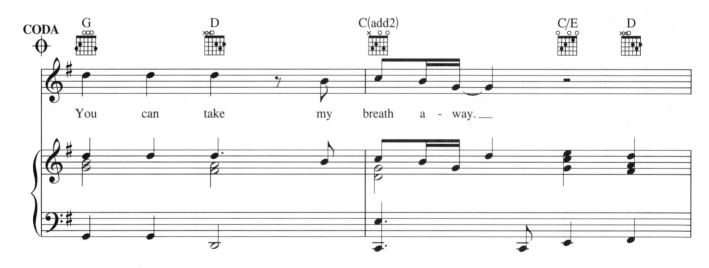

CODA

You can take my breath a - way. ___

I can be ___ your he - ro ba - by.

HOW YOU REMIND ME

Drop D tuning: ⑥ = D

Lyrics by CHAD KROEGER
Music by NICKELBACK

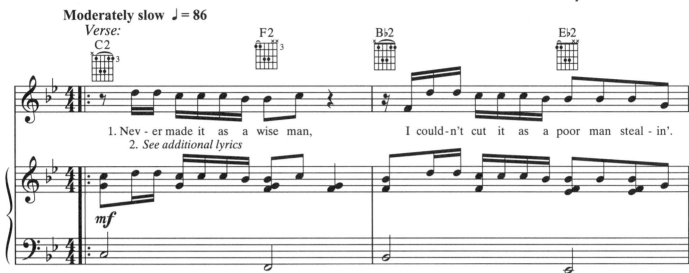

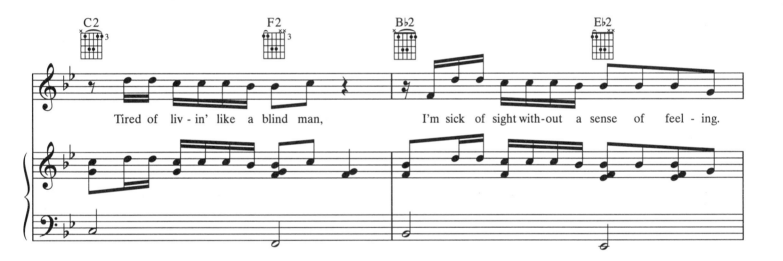

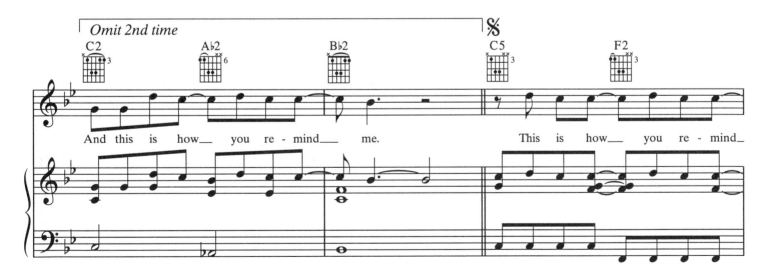

How You Remind Me - 5 - 1

Chorus:

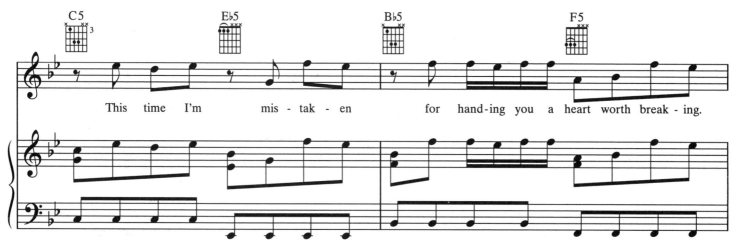

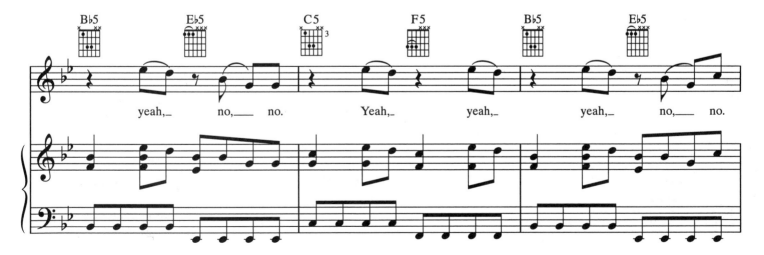

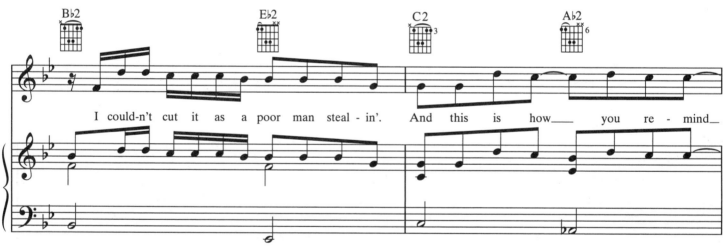

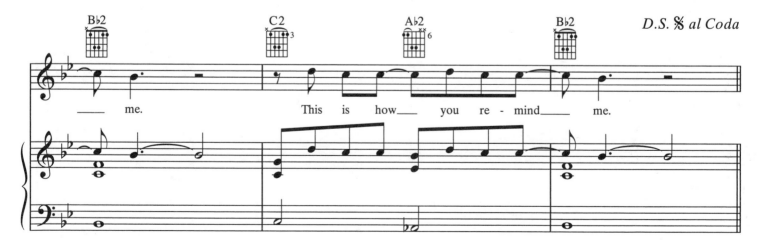

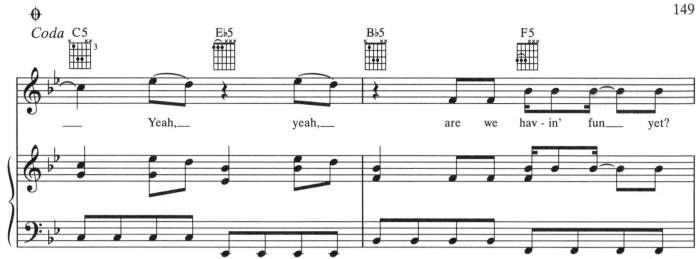

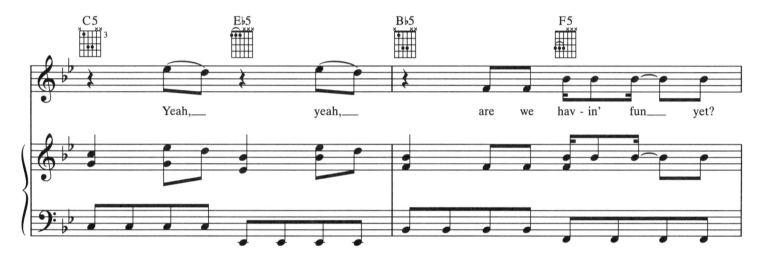

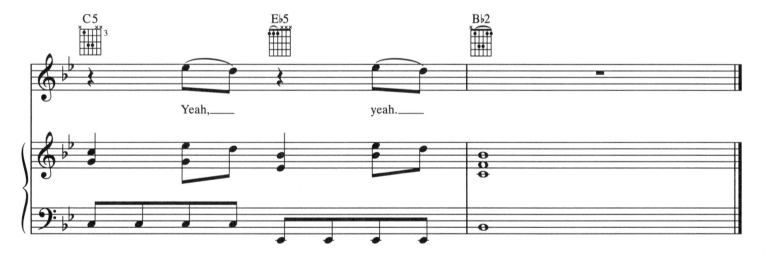

Verse 2:
It's not like you didn't know that.
I said I love you and swear I still do.
And it must have been so bad.
'Cause livin' with me must have damn near killed you.
This is how you remind me of what I really am.
This is how you remind me of what I really am.
(To Chorus:)

I CAN'T DENY IT

Words and Music by
GREGG ALEXANDER
and RICK NOWELS

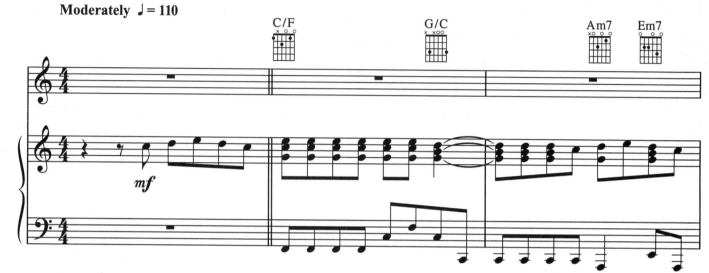

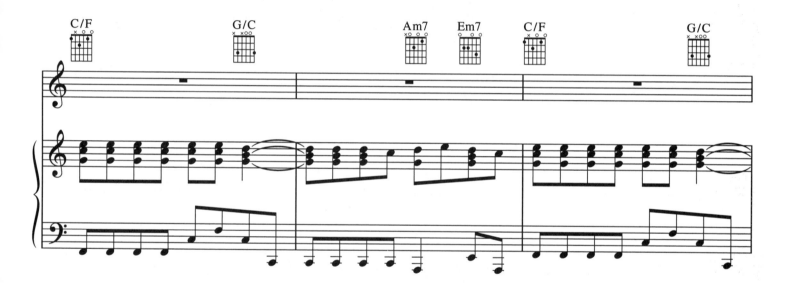

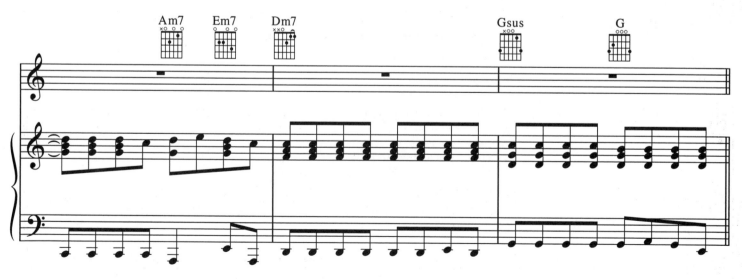

I Can't Deny It - 5 - 1

Verse:

𝄋 *Chorus:*

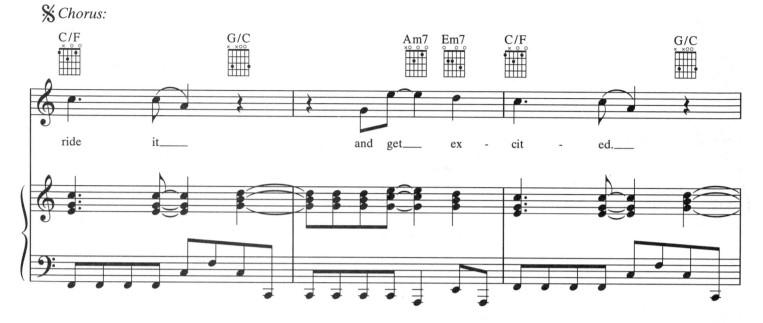

ride it___ and get___ ex - cit - ed.___

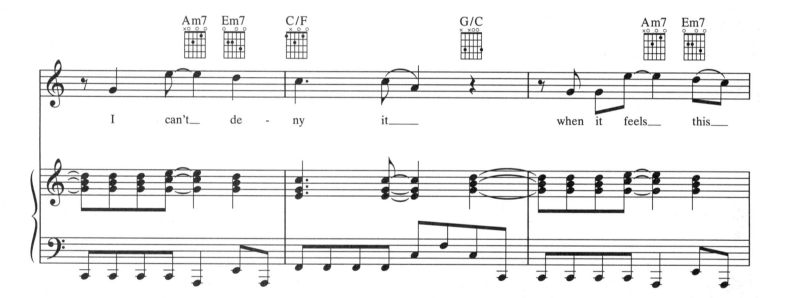

I can't___ de - ny it___ when it feels___ this___

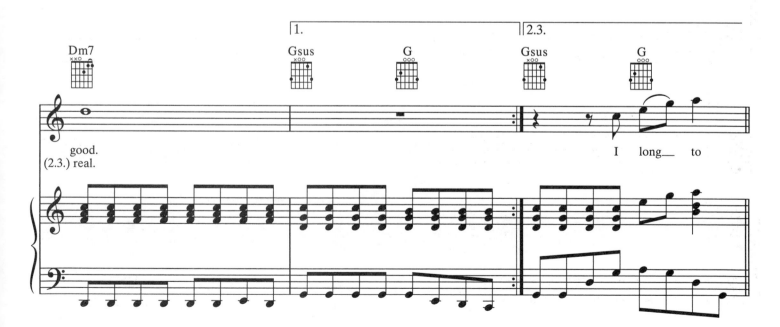

good.
(2.3.) real. I long___ to

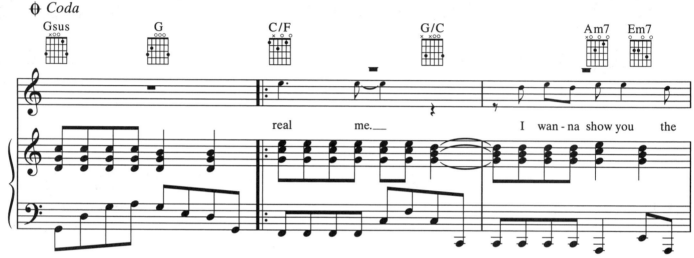

I DID IT

Words and Music by
GLEN BALLARD and DAVID JOHN MATTHEWS

Moderately ♩ = 108

Verses 1 & 2:

1. I'm mix-ing up a bunch of mag-ic stuff,
2. *See additional lyrics*

a mag-ic mush-room cloud of___ care.___ A po-tion that-'ll

I Did It - 5 - 1

% *Bridge:*

I nev-er did a sin-gle thing that did__ a sin-gle thing to change__ the ug-ly ways of the world.

I did-n't know it felt__ so right__ in - side._____ I____ did-n't know__ at all.

I o-pen up the cur - tains, I____ heard si - rens there,__ the lights flash and crawl.

I did it for jus - tice, I just did it for__ the buzz,___ y'all.

Chorus:

I did it. { Do you think I've___ gone___ too far? / I told you, I told you I did. } I did it.

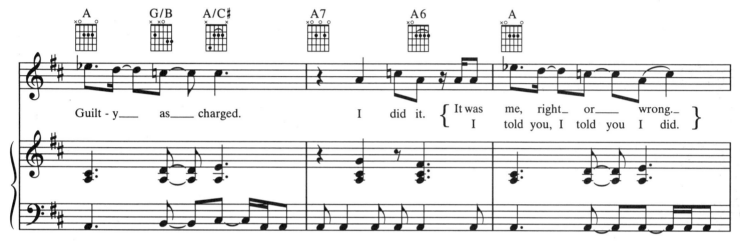

Guilt - y___ as___ charged. I did it. { It was me, right___ or___ wrong.___ / I told you, I told you I did. }

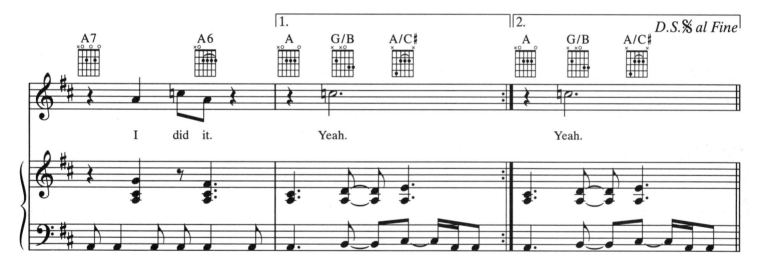

1. I did it. Yeah.

2. Yeah.

D.S.𝄋 al Fine

Verse 2:
It's a nickel or a dime for what I've done.
The truth is that I don't really care.
For such a lovely crime, I'll do the time.
You better lock me up, I'll do it again.
(To Chorus:)

Verse 4:
Go door to door, spread the love you got,
You got the love, you get what you want.
Does it matter where you get it from?
I, for one, don't turn my cheek for anyone.
Unturn your cheek to give your love, love to grow.
(To Chorus:)

I Did It - 5 - 5

I WANNA BE BAD

Words and Music by
WILLA FORD, BRIAN KIERULF
and JOSHUA M. SCHWARTZ

Moderately slow ♩ = 96

Oh,___ I, I, I.

I wan-na be bad with you ba - by. I, I, I, I,

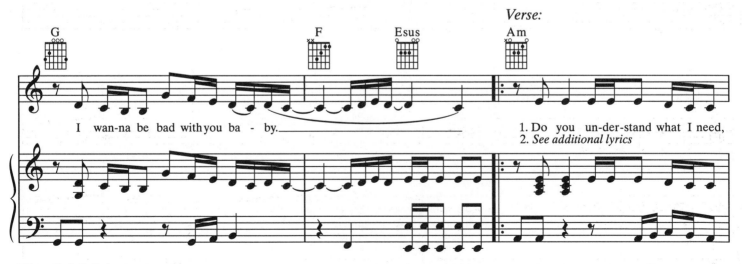

I wan-na be bad with you ba - by.___ 1. Do you un-der-stand what I need,
2. *See additional lyrics*

I Wanna Be Bad - 5 - 1

need from you? Just let me be the girl___ to show you, you, ev-'ry-thing that you can be is

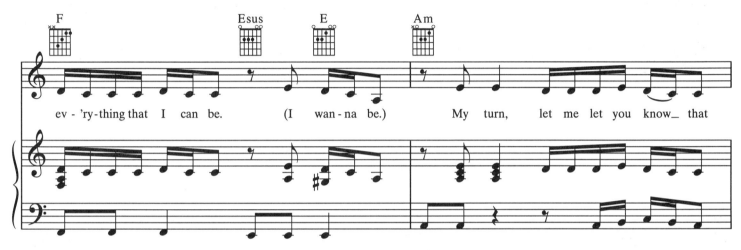

ev-'ry-thing that I can be. (I wan-na be.) My turn, let me let you know___ that

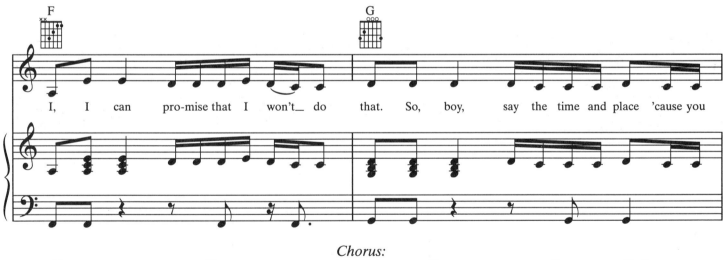

I, I can pro-mise that I won't___ do that. So, boy, say the time and place 'cause you

Chorus:

make me wan-na mis-be-have. I wan-na be bad. You make bad look so___ good. I've got things on my

rules.   'Cause I,   I   wan - na   be   bad.

Verse 2:
What's up? Tell me what to do, how to be.
Teach me all your words from A to Z.
But I don't want your other girl to see
That you're messin' 'round with me.
Should I, boy, tell you what I got is what you want?
Tell, tell me, do I, I turn you on?
I don't want no one judgin' me.
(To Chorus:)

Royce's Rap:
Willa, Willa, Willa, whatchu want, whatchu want?
Willa, Willa, Willa, whatchu want? (Come and get it from me.)
Is it him, the criminal with the Stan look?
You need the real Shady to please stand up,
Or, is it me, the criminal in the V?
And never pretend to be nothin' other than a bad boy?
If you say you want me, then tell me how you gon' be?
Hey, Royce, (Yo!) I wanna be bad.
(To Chorus:)

I WANT LOVE

Words and Music by
ELTON JOHN and BERNIE TAUPIN

I Want Love - 5 - 1

a man like me,___ so ir-res-pon-si-ble.___ A man like me is

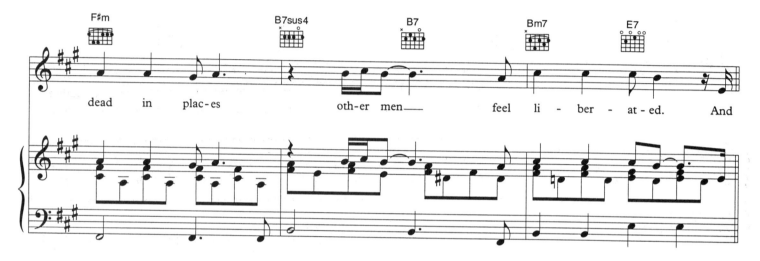

dead in plac-es oth-er men___ feel li-ber-at-ed. And

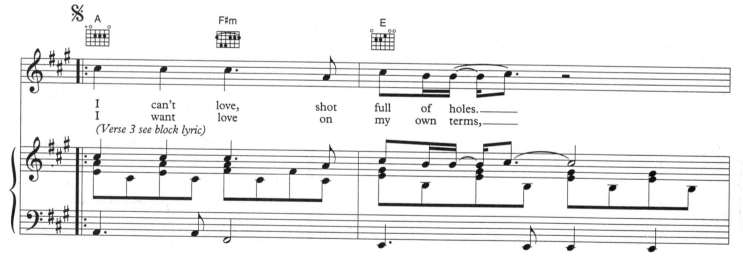

I I can't love, shot full of holes.___
I want love on my own terms,___
(Verse 3 see block lyric)

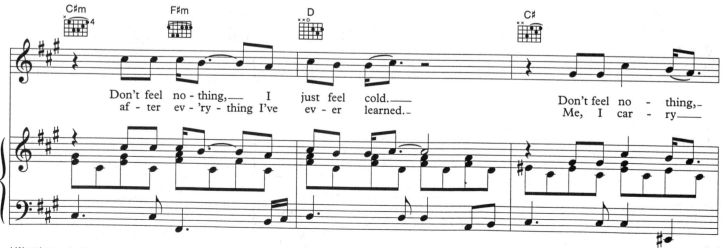

Don't feel no-thing,___ I just feel cold.___ Don't feel no thing,-
af-ter ev-'ry-thing I've ev-er learned.- Me, I car-ry

just old____ scars: tough-en-ing up   a - round   my____ heart.}
too much____ bag - gage: all that I've seen,   so   much____ traf-fic. } But

I want love,___   just a diff-'rent kind.___   I want love, won't break me down,___ won't___

brick   me   up,___   won't___ fence   me   in.___   I   want   a   love   that   don't mean a   thing;___   that's   the

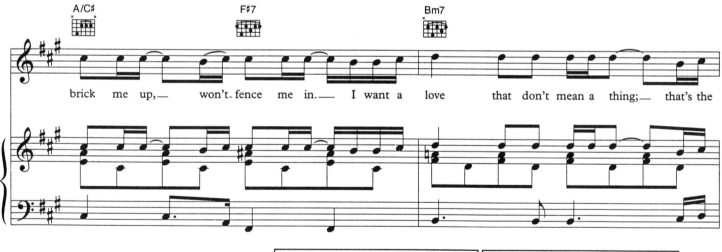

love I want.___   I____ want____ love.   love.

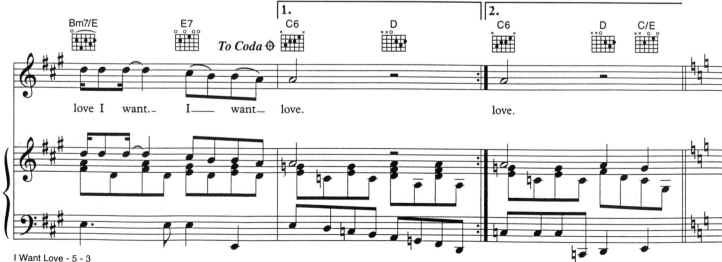

I Want Love - 5 - 3

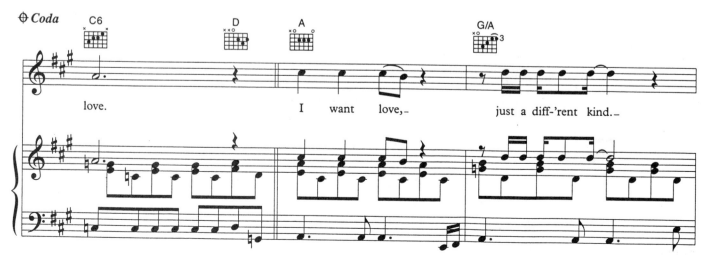

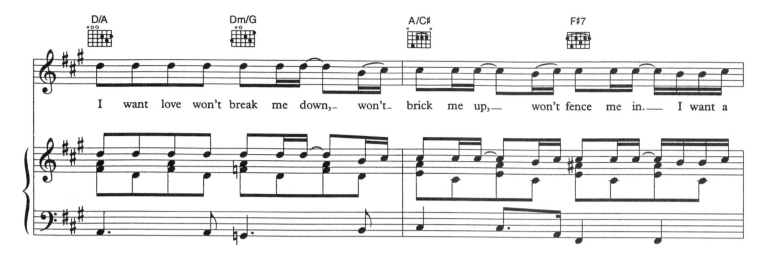

I want love won't break me down,— won't— brick me up,— won't fence me in.— I want a

love that don't mean a thing;— that's the love I want.— I— want— love.

Verse 3:
(Instrumental)
A man like me is dead in places
Other men feel liberated.

And I want love *etc.*

I'M ALREADY THERE

Words and Music by
GARY BAKER, FRANK J. MYERS
and RICHIE McDONALD

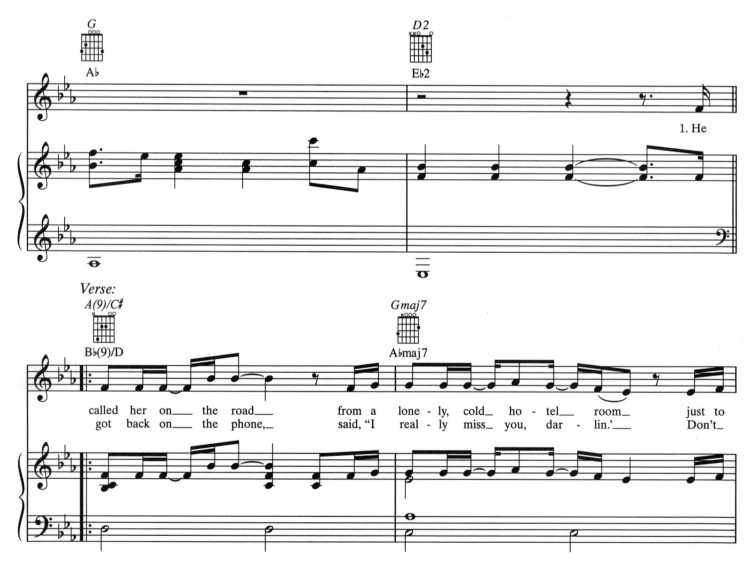

I'm Already There - 5 - 1

first thing that came to his mind.____ I'm al - read - y there.____
out the light and close your eyes."____ I'm al - read - y there.____

Chorus:

1.3. Take a look a - round.____ I'm the sun - shine in your
2. Don't make a sound.____ I'm the beat in your

hair. I'm the sha - dow on the ground.____ I'm the whis - per in the wind.__
heart. I'm the moon - light shin - ing down.____ I'm the whis - per in the wind.__

(1.) I'm your i - mag - i - nar - y friend.____ And I know____
(2.3.) And I'll be there 'til the end.____ Can you feel____

I'M LIKE A BIRD

Words and Music by
NELLY FURTADO

I'm Like a Bird - 5 - 3

178

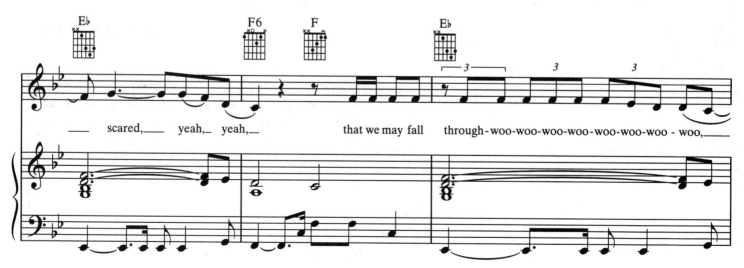

I'm Like a Bird - 5 - 4

I'm Like a Bird - 5 - 5

IF MY HEART HAD WINGS

Tune guitar down a half step:
⑥ = E♭ ③ = G♭
⑤ = A♭ ② = B♭
④ = D♭ ① = E♭

Words and Music by
J. FRED KNOBLOCH and
ANNIE ROBOFF

If My Heart Had Wings - 6 - 1

If my heart had wings.

Verse 2:
Who poured this pain?
Who made these clouds?
I stare through this windshield
Thinkin' out loud.
Time keeps on crawling,
Love keeps on calling me home.

Verse 3:
We both committed.
We both agreed.
You do what you have to
To get what you need.
Feeling you near me
With so many miles in between,
Oh, Lord, it ain't easy
Out here in the dark
To keep us together so far apart.
(To Chorus:)

IRRESISTIBLE

Words and Music by
PAM SHEYNE, ARNTHOR BIRGISSON
and ANDERS SVEN BAGGE

Moderately ♩ = 94

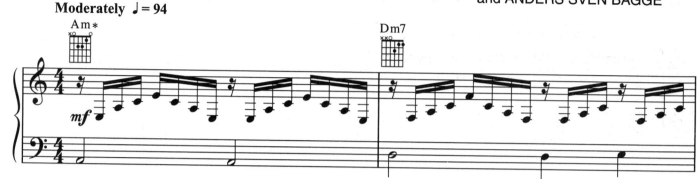

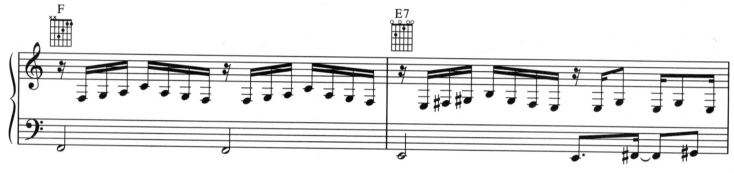

Ooh,_____

Spoken: You know, I don't know what it is...

Yeah,___ yeah,___ yeah,___ yeah,___ yeah.___

but everything about you is so irresistible.

*Original recording in G♯ minor

Irresistible - 6 - 1

Verse:

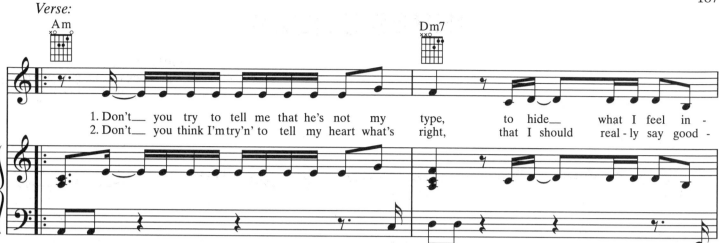

1. Don't__ you try to tell me that he's not my type, to hide__ what I feel in -
2. Don't__ you think I'm tryn' to tell my heart what's right, that I should real - ly say good -

side, when he makes me weak with__ de - si - re.
night? But I just can't stop my - self fall - ing.__

I____ know that I'm__ sup - posed to make him wait, let__ him think I like the
May - be I'll tell__ him that I feel the same, that I don't wan - na play no

chase,__ but I can't stop fan - ning__ the fi - re.__
game.__ 'Cause when I feel stop his arms wrapped__ a - round me....__

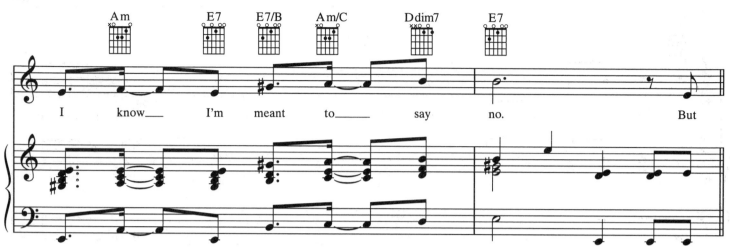

I know___ I'm meant to___ say no. But

Chorus:

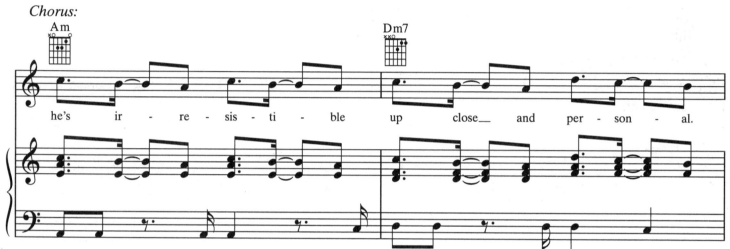

he's ir - re - sis - ti - ble up close___ and per - son - al.

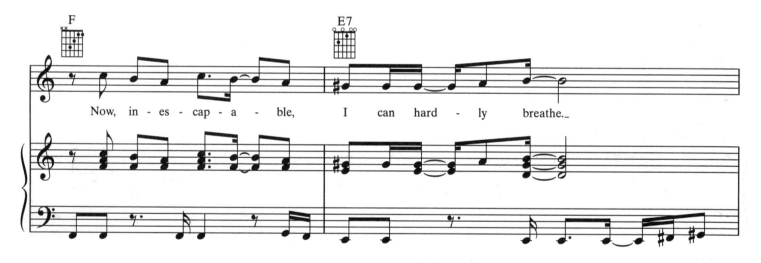

Now, in - es - cap - a - ble, I can hard - ly breathe.___

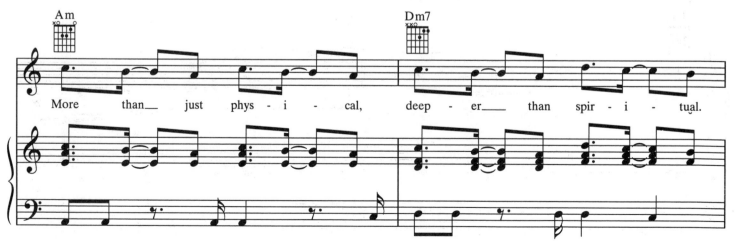

More than___ just phys - i - cal, deep - er___ than spir - i - tual.

His ways are pow-er-ful, ir-re-sis-ti-ble__ to me.__

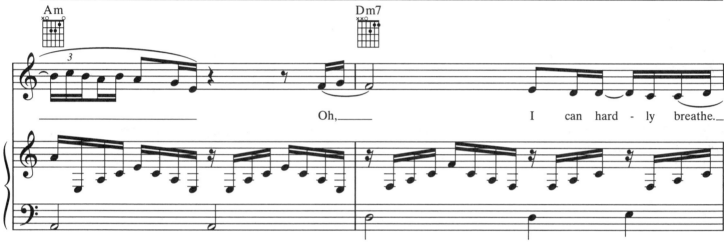

Oh,__ I can hard-ly breathe.__

Yeah,__ yeah,__ yeah,__ yeah,__ yeah.__

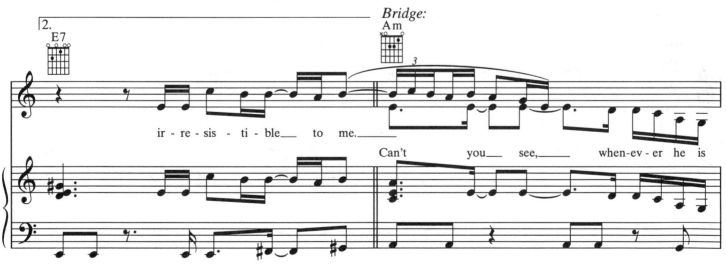

ir-re-sis-ti-ble__ to me.__ Can't you__ see,__ when-ev-er he is

close to___ me,___ I real-ly find it hard to___ breathe?___ He's

so ir - re - sis - ti - ble. Think he___ knows,___ it's more than just

spir - i - tual.___ His kiss-es are___ pow - er - ful.___ He's

He's so ir - re - sis - ti - ble._____
so ir - re - sis - ti - ble.

Chorus:

He's ir - re - sis - ti - ble up close__ and per - son - al.

Now, in - es - cap - a - ble, I can hard - ly breathe.__

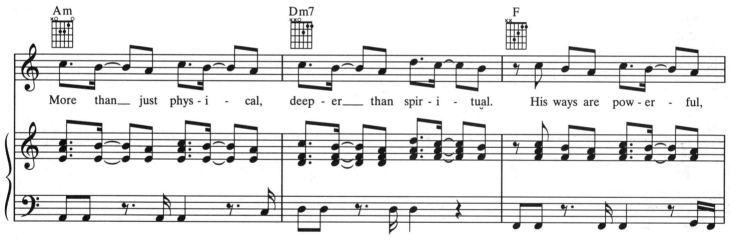

More than__ just phys - i - cal, deep - er__ than spir - i - tual. His ways are pow - er - ful,

ir - re - sis - ti - ble__ to me.__ ir - re - sis - ti - ble__ to me.__

IT'S BEEN AWHILE

Slow rock ♩ = 58

Words and Music by
AARON LEWIS, MICHAEL MUSHOK,
JONATHAN WYSOCKI and JOHN APRIL

1. And it's been a while
2.3. *See additional lyrics*

It's Been Awhile - 6 - 1

Outro:

Coda

And it's been a-while since I____ could hold____ my head____ up high.____ And it's been a while since I____ said I'm sor-ry.

Verse 2:
And it's been a while since I could say that I wasn't addicted.
And it's been a while since I could say I loved myself as well.
And it's been a while since I've gone and f***ed thing up just like I always do.
And it's been a while, but all that sh** seems to disappear when I'm with you.
(To Chorus:)

Verse 3:
And it's been a while since I could look at myself straight.
And it's been a while since I said I'm sorry.
And it's been a while since I've seen the way the candles light your face.
And it's been a while, but I can still remember just the way you taste.

Last Chorus:
And everything I can't remember,
As f***ed up as it all may seem to be, I know it's me.
I cannot blame this on my father.
He did the best he could for me.
(To Outro:)

IT HAPPENS EVERY TIME

Music and Lyrics by
JÖRGEN ELOFSSON

It Happens Every Time - 5 - 1

Verses 2 & 3:

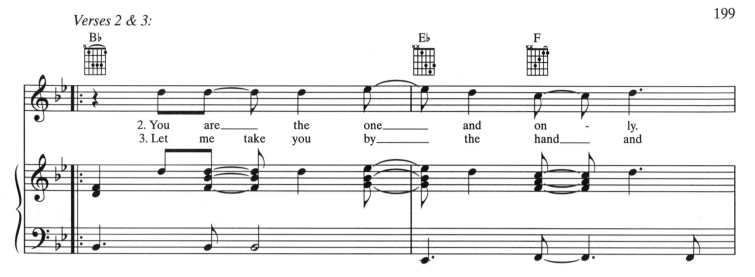

2. You are ___ the one ___ and on ___ ly.
3. Let me take you by ___ the hand ___ and

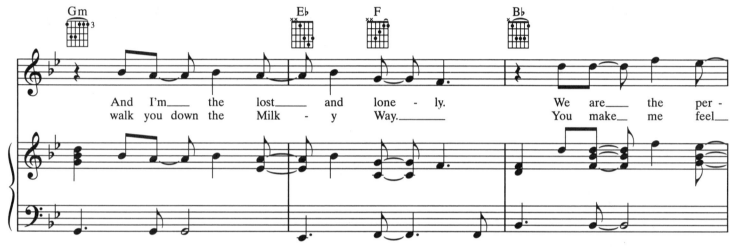

And I'm ___ the lost ___ and lone ___ ly. We are ___ the per-
walk you down the Milk ___ y Way. ___ You make ___ me feel ___

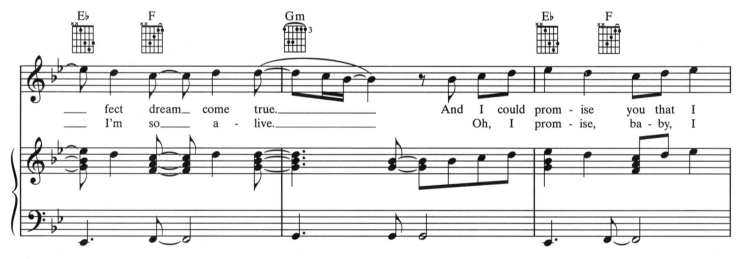

___ fect dream ___ come true. ___ And I could prom-ise you that I
___ I'm so ___ a - live. ___ Oh, I prom-ise, ba-by, I

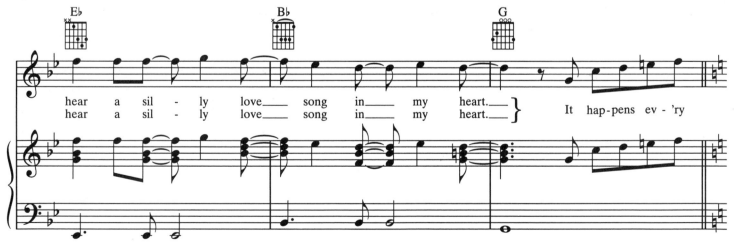

hear a sil - ly love ___ song in ___ my heart. ___
hear a sil - ly love ___ song in ___ my heart. ___ It hap-pens ev - 'ry

Chorus:

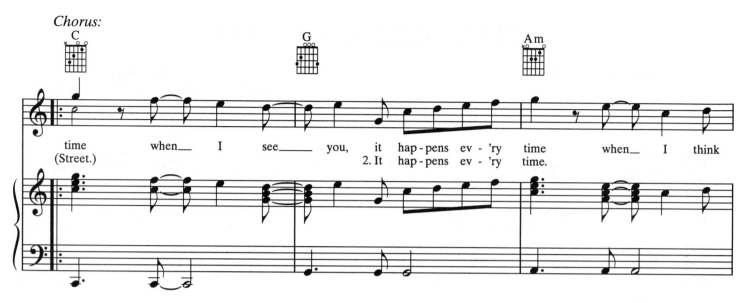

time when__ I see_____ you, it hap-pens ev - 'ry time when__ I think
(Street.) 2. It hap-pens ev - 'ry time.

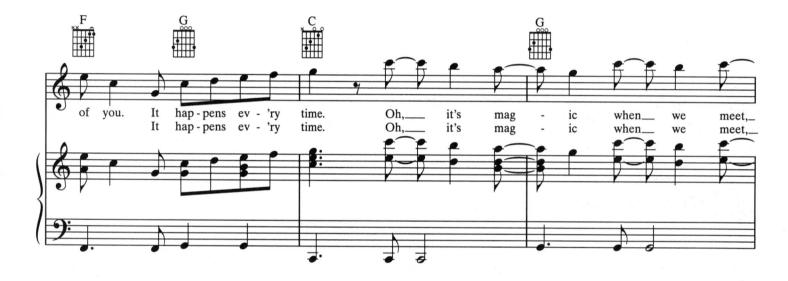

of you. It hap-pens ev - 'ry time. Oh,__ it's mag - ic when__ we meet,__
It hap-pens ev - 'ry time. Oh,__ it's mag - ic when__ we meet,__

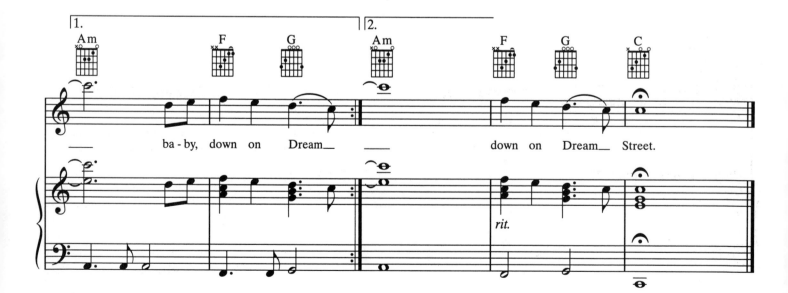

ba - by, down on Dream__ __ down on Dream__ Street.

rit.

JUST ANOTHER GIRL

Moderately ♩ = 96

Verse:

Words and Music by
DAMON SHARPE, CARSTEN LINDBERG,
JOACHIM SVARE and LINDY ROBBINS

1. You think you're slick in ev - 'ry way, chang-in' the codes__ on your phone ev-'ry day.__
2. Strange, how you claim to tell__ the truth, when the pas-sen-ger seat__ in your car's been moved.__

Is there some-thing that__ you're try'n'__ to hide__ from me?__
And you swore that there__ was no__ one else__ but you.__

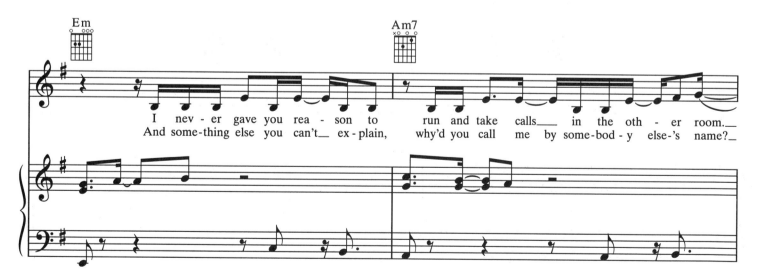

I nev-er gave you rea-son to run and take calls__ in the oth-er room.__
And some-thing else you can't__ ex-plain, why'd you call me by some-bod-y else's name?__

Just Another Girl - 5 - 1

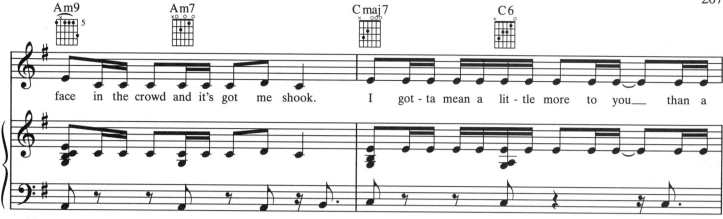

face in the crowd and it's got me shook. I got-ta mean a lit-tle more to you___ than a

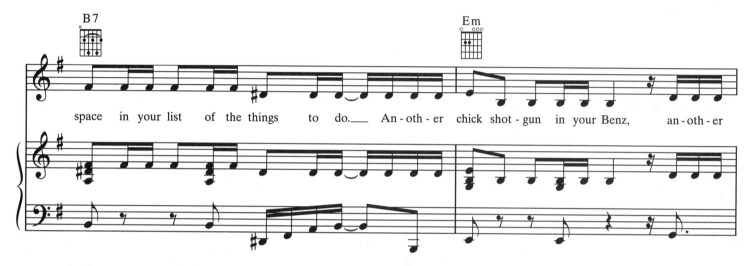

space in your list of the things to do.___ An-oth-er chick shot-gun in your Benz, an-oth-er

dime piece that you can show all your friends. You can call me cra-zy, say I'm in-se-cure,___ but

I don't wan-na be just an-oth-er girl. I don't wan-na be just an-oth-er girl.___
Just an-oth-er

GOD BLESS THE U.S.A.

Words and Music by
LEE GREENWOOD

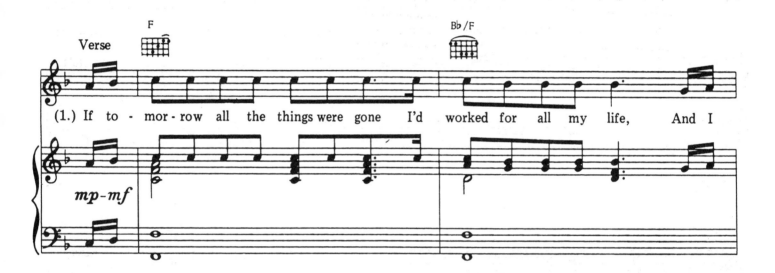

God Bless the U.S.A. - 5 - 1

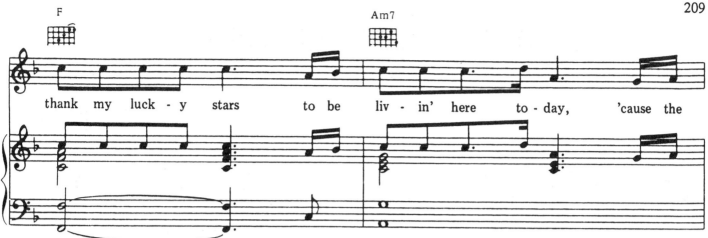

stand up; next to you and de - fend her still to - day. 'Cause there

ain't no doubt I love this land _____ God bless the U S

A

(2.) From the

Verse

lakes of Min - ne - so - ta, to the hills of Ten - nes - see, ___ a -

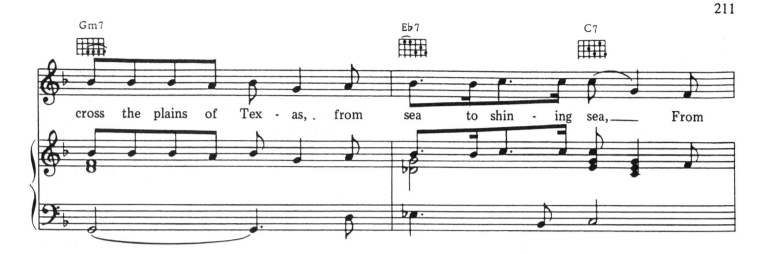

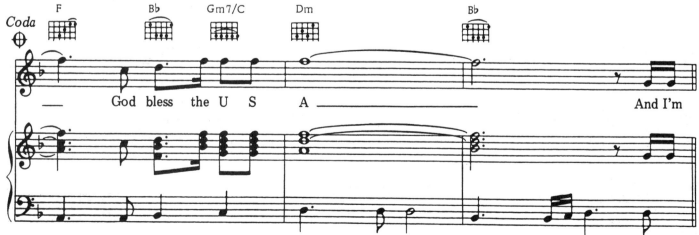

God Bless the U.S.A. - 5 - 4

Chorus

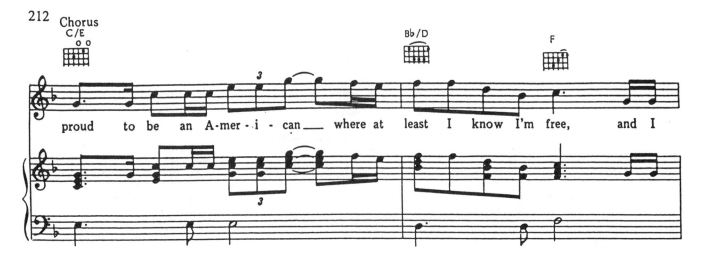

LIQUID DREAMS

Words and Music by
BRADLEY SPALTER, JOSHUA THOMPSON,
MICHAEL NORFLEET and QUINCY PATRICK

Verse:

1. Post - ers of love__ sur - round - ing__ me,__ lost in the world__ of fan -
2. *See additional lyrics*

ta - sy.__ Ev - er - y night__ she comes__ to me and gives me

Pre-Chorus:

all the love___ I need._____ Now this hot girl, she's

not your av-'rage girl. She's a morph-a-rot-ic dream from a mag-a-zine.___ And she's___

___ so fine, de-signed to blow your mind. She's a dom-in-a-trix sup-er-mod-el

Chorus:

beau-ty queen.___ I dream a-bout a girl___ who's a mix of Des-

Repeat ad lib. and fade

Verse 2:
Angelina Jolie's lips to kiss in the dark
Underneath Cindy C's beauty mark.
When it comes to the test, well, Tyra's the best
And Salma Hayek brings the rest.
(To Pre-Chorus:)

LADY
(HEAR ME TONIGHT)

Words and Music by
BERNARD EDWARDS, NILE RODGERS,
YANN DESTAGNOL and ROMAIN TRANCHART

La-dy,___ hear___ me to-night,___ 'cause___ my

Lady (Hear Me Tonight) - 4 - 1

221

Lady (Hear Me Tonight) - 4 - 4

LOVE DON'T COST A THING

Words and Music by
DAMON SHARPE, GREG LAWSON,
GEORGETTE FRANKLIN, JEREMY MONROE
and APRIL HARRIS

Am7

thing. Think I wan-na drive your Benz, I don't. If I wan-na floss, I got my

Em7

To Coda

own.____ E - ven if you were broke,_ my love don't cost a

Verse:
Am7

thing. 1. When you rolled up in____ the Es - ca -lade, saw the dub you gave to the va - let.
2. *See additional lyrics*

Em7

Knew that it was game when you looked at me, pull-in' up your sleeve so I can see the Ro - lie bling.

Verse 2:
When I took a chance, thought you'd understand,
Baby, credit cards aren't romance.
Still, you're tryin' to buy what's already yours.
What I need from you is not available in stores.
Seen a side of you that I really feel.
You're doin' way too much; never keep it real.
If it doesn't change, gotta hit the road.
Now I'm leavin'. Where's my keys? I've got to go.
(To Pre-Chorus:)

LOVE OF MY LIFE

Words and Music by
BRIAN McKNIGHT

*Original recording in Gb major.
**Sung falsetto.

Love of My Life - 5 - 1

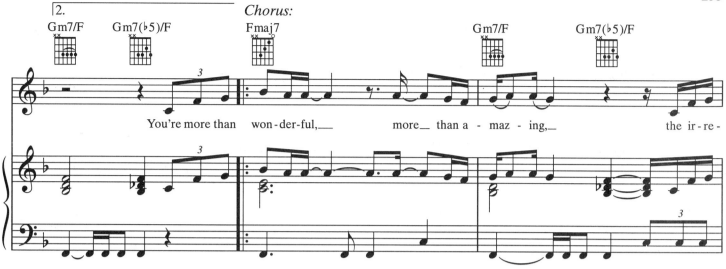

You're more than won-der-ful,__ more__ than a - maz - ing,__ the ir - re -

place - a - ble_____ love__ of my life. You're so in - cred - i - ble__ here in these

Repeat ad lib. and fade

arms to - night,__ the ir - re - place - a - ble_____ love__ of my life.

Verse 2:
Always seems like a reality.
Forever don't seem so far away.
All I wanna do,
All I wanna feel,
All I wanna be
Is close to you.
Every day is my lucky day.
All I wanna do is love you.
I place no other above you.
I'll tell you why...
(To Chorus:)

LOVERBOY

Words and Music by
LARRY BLACKMON, TOMI JENKINS
and MARIAH CAREY

wan-na, I wan-na, I wan-na, I wan-na, I need a, I need a, I need a, I need a, a

Loverboy - 7 - 1

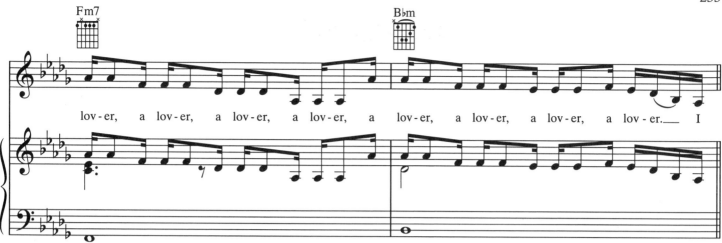

lov-er, a lov-er, a lov-er, a lov-er, a lov-er, a lov-er, a lov-er, a lov-er.___ I

Verse:

got my-self a lov - er___ who knows_what I like._____ When
2. *See additional lyrics*

he in-vites me o - ver,___ I come ev-'ry time._____ Oh,

when my sug - ar dad - dy___ takes me for a ride,_____ wher -

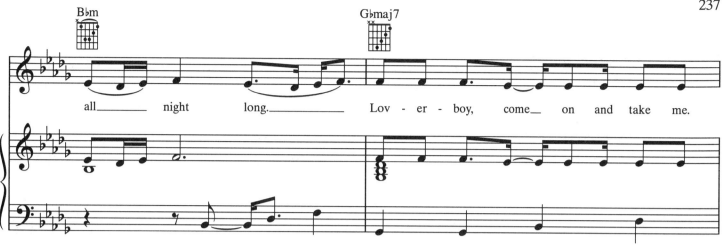

all_____ night long._____ Lov - er - boy, come__ on and take me.

On - ly you know__ how to make me shud - der with an - ti - ci - pa - tion

1.

all_____ night long._____

2.

all_____ night long._____ This

Bridge:

N.C.

stuff is start - ing now.__ This stuff is start - ing now.__ It's the same feel - ing I

Verse 2:
Got myself a lover and he's so sublime.
It's quite a bit of heaven to feel him inside
'Cause when my sugar daddy takes me for a ride,
Whatever way we go is delirium time.
I get weak when his candy kisses sweetly
Caress my whole body.
All I need is him to be my loverboy.
(To Chorus:)

MISSING YOU

Words and Music by
JOE THOMAS, JOSHUA THOMPSON,
TIM KELLY and BOB ROBINSON

Moderately slow ♩ = 86

1. Stand-ing here,___ look-ing out my win - dow.___ The
2. Driv-ing 'round,___ thought I saw you pass___ me.___ My

nights are long____ and my days are cold____ 'cause I don't have you.____
rear - view mir-ror's play-ing tricks on me____ 'cause you fade a - way.____

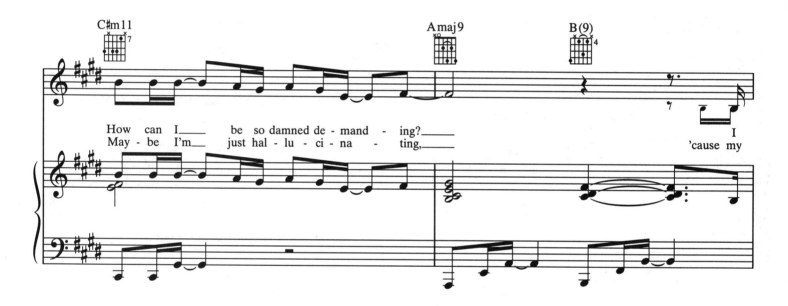

How can I____ be so damned de - mand - ing?____ I
May - be I'm____ just hal - lu - ci - na - ting,____ 'cause my

know you said____ that it's o - ver now,____ but I can't let____ go.____ } Ev - 'ry
lone - li - ness____ got the best of me____ and my heart's so____ weak.____ } Ev - 'ry

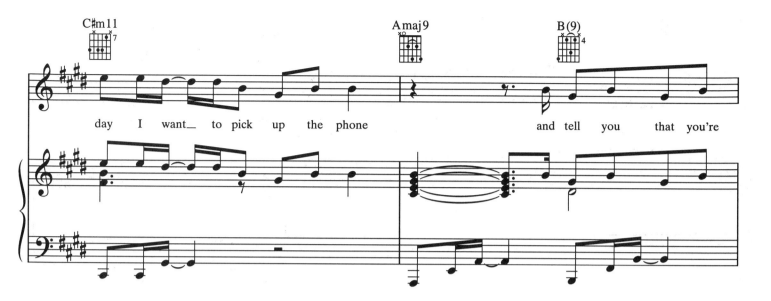

day I want_ to pick up the phone and tell you that you're

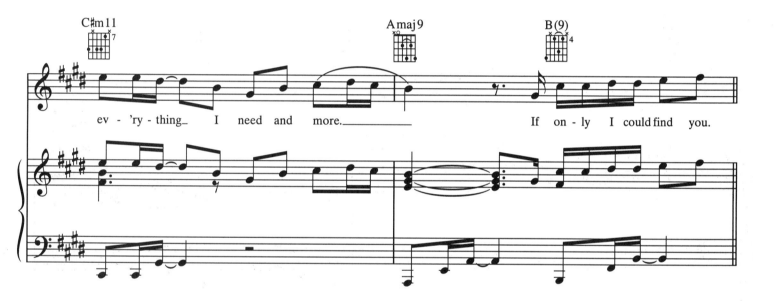

ev - 'ry - thing_ I need and more._____ If on - ly I could find you.

𝄉 Chorus:

Like a cold_ sum-mer af - ter - noon,_____ like the snow_ com-ing down in June,_

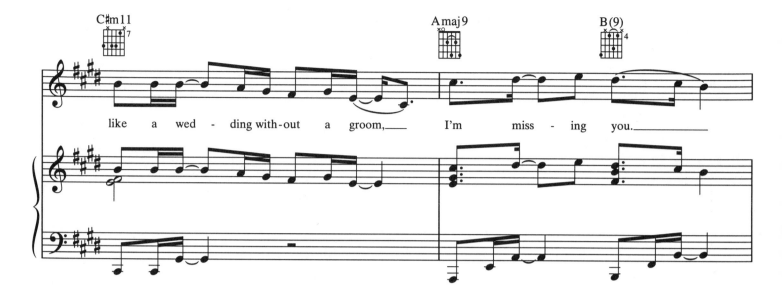

like a wed - ding with-out a groom,___ I'm miss - ing you.___

I'm the des - ert with-out the sand.___ You're the wom - an with-out a man.___

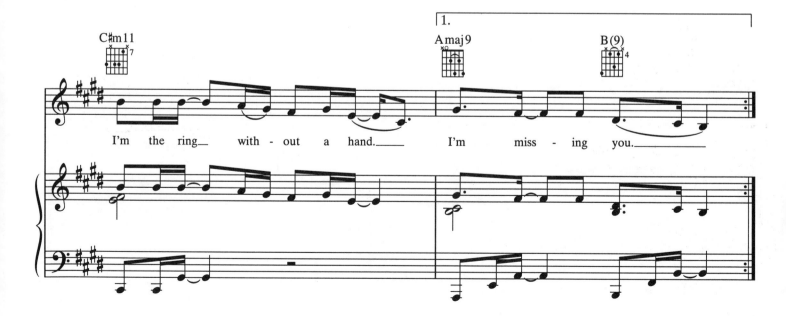

1.

I'm the ring___ with - out a hand.___ I'm miss - ing you.___

I'm miss - ing you.____ I'm miss - ing you.____

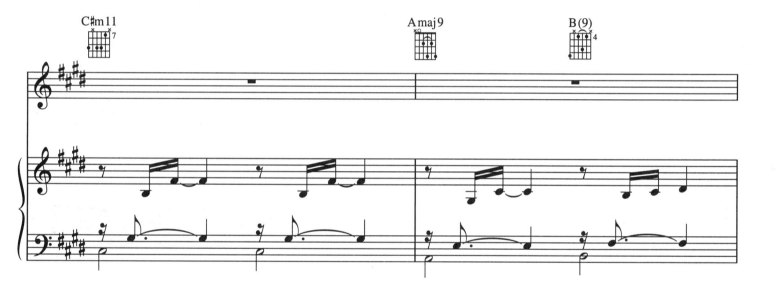

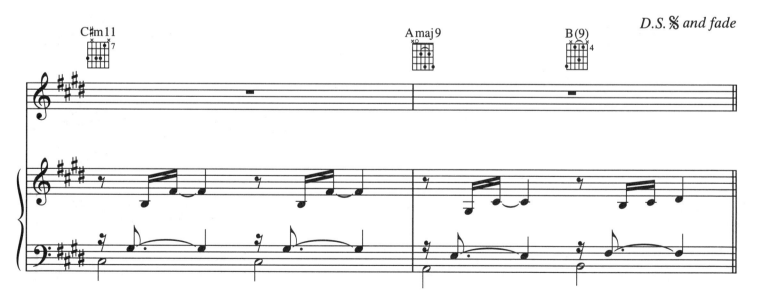

MISS ME SO BAD

Words and Music by
DIANE WARREN

I will get in-to your heart, I will get in-to your

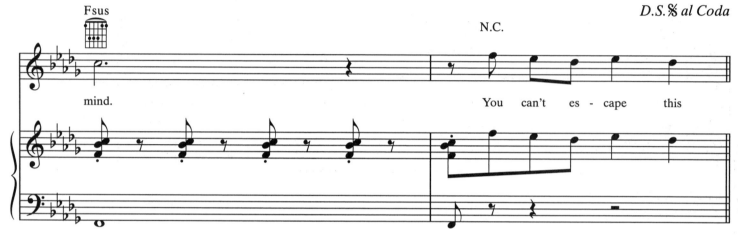

mind. You can't es-cape this

D.S. % al Coda

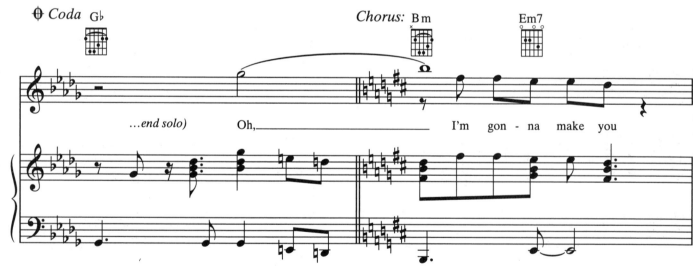

...end solo) Oh,_____ I'm gon-na make you

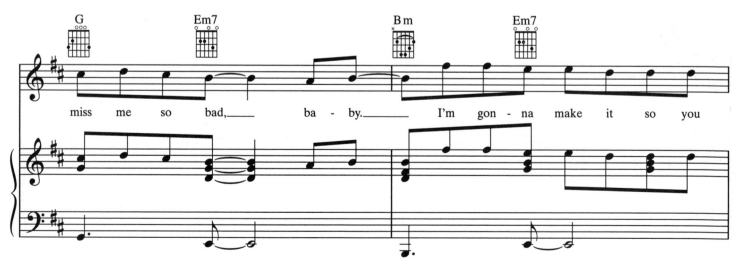

miss me so bad,___ ba-by._____ I'm gon-na make it so you

can't get e-nough of my love.___ I'm gon-na make sure ev-'ry

night you dream of my touch,___ un-til you're touch-ing me, un-til you're touch-ing me a-gain.

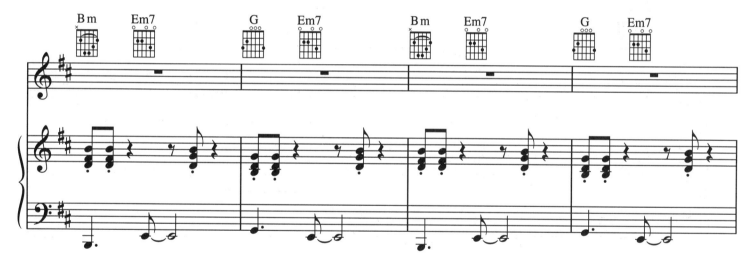

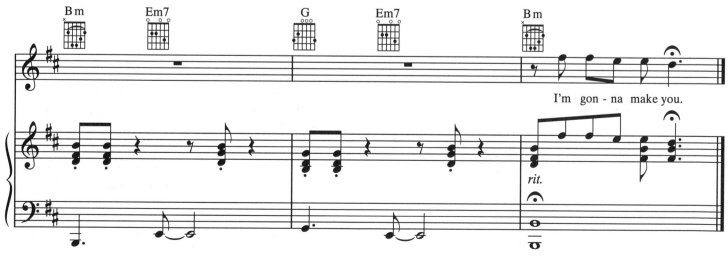

I'm gon-na make you.

rit.

MORE THAN THAT

Words and Music by
FRANCIZ & LePONT and ADAM ANDERS

Moderately, with a double-time beat ♩ = 80

Verse 1:

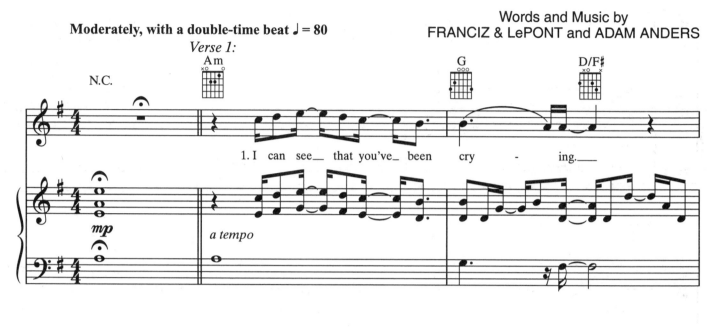

1. I can see__ that you've__ been cry - ing.__

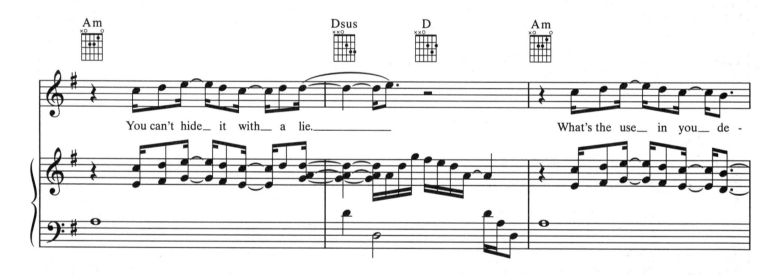

You can't hide__ it with__ a lie.__ What's the use__ in you__ de-

ny - ing__ that what__ you have__ is wrong?__

Verses 2 & 3:

No More
(BABY I'MA DO RIGHT)

Words and Music by
S. HALL, N. BUTLER
and C. GILES

Verse:

get-ting a lit-tle tir-ed of your bro-ken prom-is-es, prom-is-es, look-ing at your pag-er, see-ing dif-f'rent num-bers and num-bers.
treat me like a la-dy when you o-pen door and doors. But then you wan-na front when you wit your boys, your boys.

Call you on you cell, you're hang-in' with the fel-las, the fel-las. Hang-in' with my girls, you al-ways get-tin' jeal-ous 'n' jeal-ous.
How you gon-na play me when I bought yo clothes, yo clothes. The ones that you'll be wear-in' when you wit yo does, yo does. You

No More (Baby I'ma Do Right) - 6 - 1

No More (Baby I'ma Do Right) - 6 - 2

𝄋 *Chorus:*

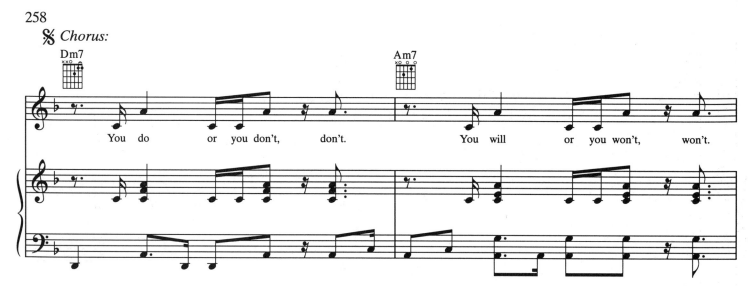

You do or you don't, don't. You will or you won't, won't.

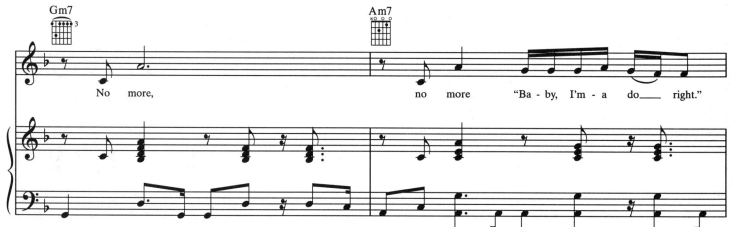

No more, no more "Ba - by, I'm - a do____ right."

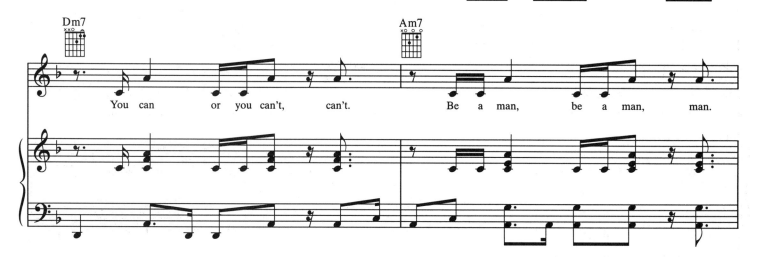

You can or you can't, can't. Be a man, be a man, man.

1.

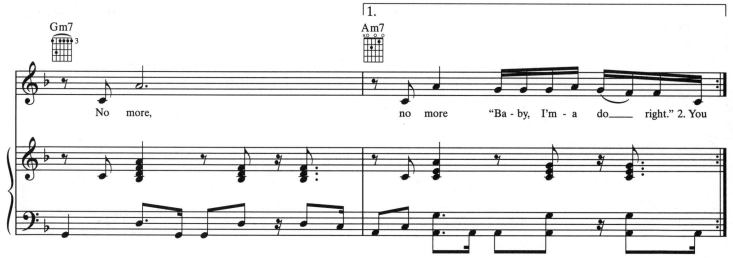

No more, no more "Ba - by, I'm - a do____ right." 2. You

NOBODY WANTS TO BE LONELY

Words and Music by
DESMOND CHILD, VICTORIA SHAW
and GARY BURR

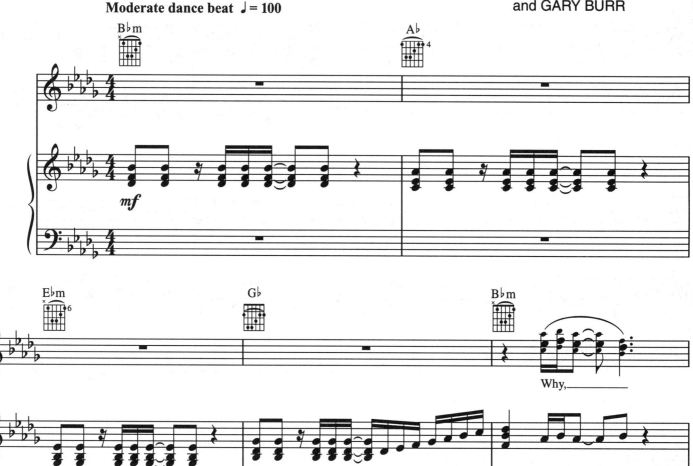

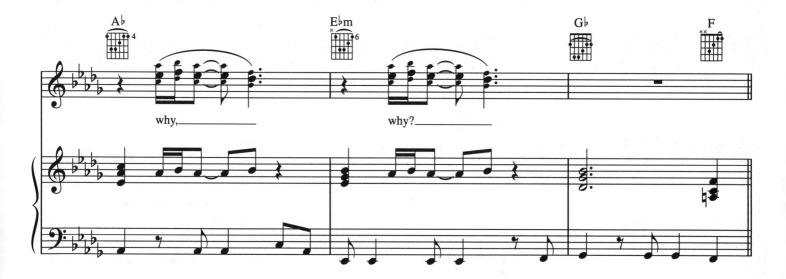

Nobody Wants to Be Lonely - 6 - 1

Verse:

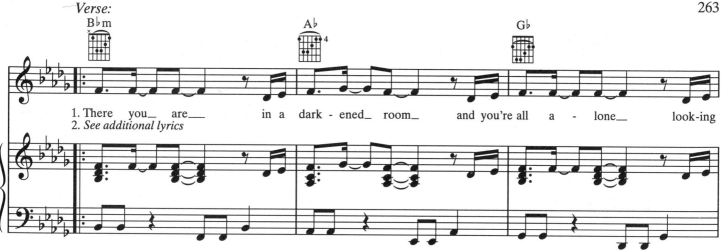

1. There you__ are__ in a dark-ened__ room__ and you're all a - lone__ look-ing
2. *See additional lyrics*

out the win - dow. Your heart is cold and lost__ the will__ to love,__

__ like a bro-ken__ ar - row. Here I stand in__ the

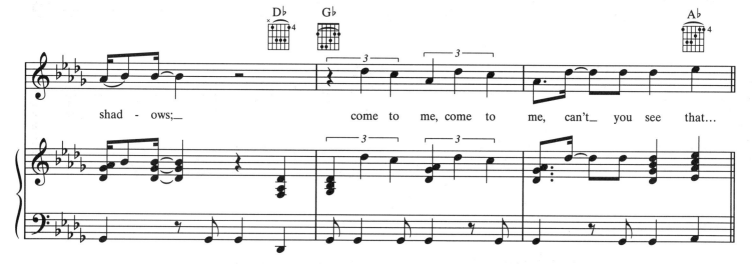

shad - ows;__ come to me, come to me, can't__ you see that...

𝄋 Chorus:

No - bod - y wants__ to be lone - ly, no - bod - y wants__

__ to cry.__ My bod - y's long - ing to hold__ you

so bad, it hurts__ in - side.__ *cresc.* Time is pre - cious and it's *f*

slip - ping a - way, and I've been wait - ing for you all of__ my__ life. *dim.*

To Coda ⊕

No - bod - y wants___ to be lone - ly, so why,_____

1.

Why don't you let___ me love___ you? why,_____

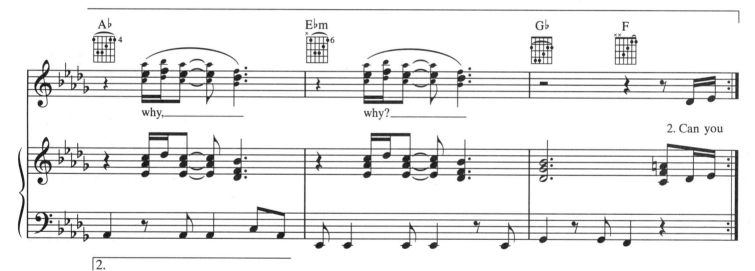

why,_____ why?_____

2. Can you

2.

Why don't you let___ me love___ you?___

I___ wan-na feel___ you need_ me

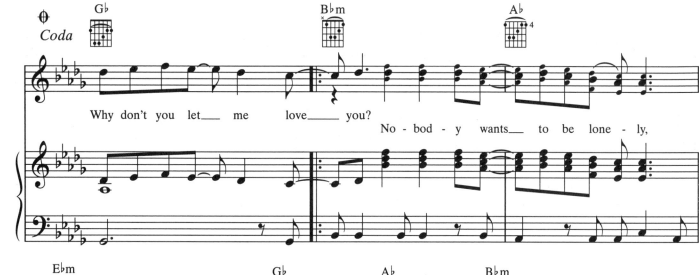

Repeat ad lib. and fade

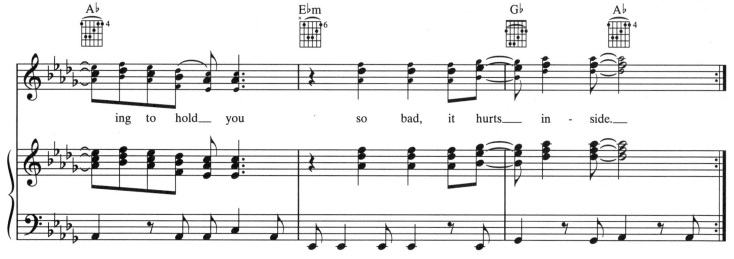

Verse 2:
Can you hear my voice?
Do you hear my song?
It's a serenade
So your heart can find me.
And suddenly you're flying down the stairs
Into my arms, baby.
Before I start going crazy,
Run to me, run to me
'Cause I'm dyin'.
(To Chorus:)

OH AARON

Words and Music by
ANDY GOLDMARK, JOSHUA M. SCHWARTZ
and BRIAN KIERULF

Moderately ♩ = 96

Well, I guess the best way___ for me to be-gin___ is... the oth-er day,___ I was hang-ing with some friends, go-in' a-round the room, talk-in' 'bout our fa-v'rite noise. I said I had a broth-er in the Back-street Boys. So

Oh Aaron - 5 - 1

"By the way, Aa-ron, if you could while you're at it, can you hook up some seats__ for my friends and my par-ents?" "So I

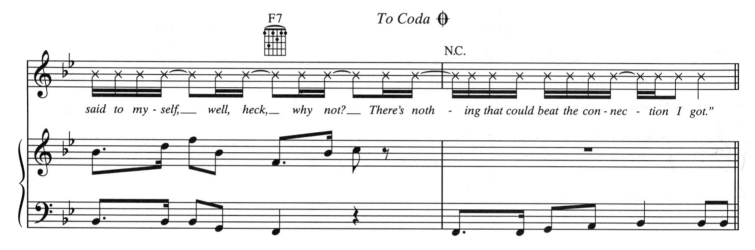

To Coda ⊕

said to my-self,__ well, heck,__ why not?__ There's noth - ing that could beat the con - nec - tion I got."

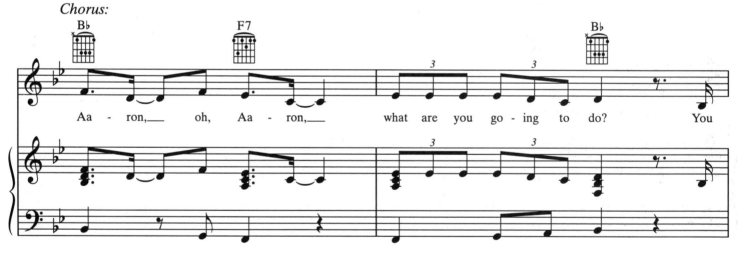

Chorus:

Aa - ron,__ oh, Aa - ron,__ what are you go - ing to do? You

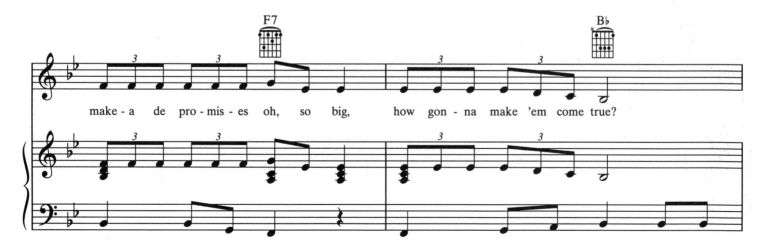

make - a de pro - mis - es oh, so big, how gon - na make 'em come true?

Repeat ad lib. and fade

Verse 2:
"Hello?"
"Hey, Nick, I need a favor from you, dude,
I promised people tickets, so you gotta come through."
"Sure, bro, how many do you need?"
"One, two, uh, three thousand three."
"What? I can get you maybe a dozen.
You can't promise seats to everyone and their cousin.
What did you do? How'd you get into this mess?"
"I was talkin' to this girl…"
"Hold your breath, I know the rest.
I guess you better get yourself a whole lotta money."
"For three thousand tickets, Nick? That isn't funny.
How'm I s'posed to pull that off in so little time?"
"You got me, Aaron, that's your problem, not mine."
(To Chorus:)

Verse 3:
How in the world could he do that to me?
I thought we were blood, I thought we were family.
We're gettin' to that show, we'll get good seats.
Everyone on the bus, y'all comin' with me.
I'm telling you guys, when we get to the gate,
He can never say no when he looks at my face.
"Hook me up, Nick, man, I swear I'll pay you back."
"Well, come to think about it, we need an opening act."
"What do you want me to do, tell jokes, dance, act?"
"Nah, I want you on stage. I want you to rap.
'Cuz if you don't, you're gonna have some disappointed friends.
And by the way, you're on at 8, that's when the show begins."
(To Chorus:)

"Now, opening up for the Backstreet Boys,
Give it up for… Aaron Carter!"

PLAY

Words and Music by
**ARNTHOR BIRGISSON,
ANDERS SVEN BAGGE, CHRISTINA MILIAN
and COREY ROONEY**

Moderately ♩ = 106

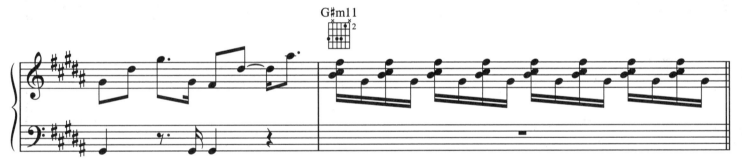

Verse:
N.C.

1. I could wait all night and day to go to a par-ty, sit down and wait.
2. *See additional lyrics*

Play - 7 - 1

Give my re-quest to the D. J. 'cause my song he's got-ta play.

And when I hear that beat, I get my bod-y up out my seat,

G#m11

I grab a guy and move my feet. He's play-in' my___ song.___

%. *Chorus:*

G#m7   F#/G#

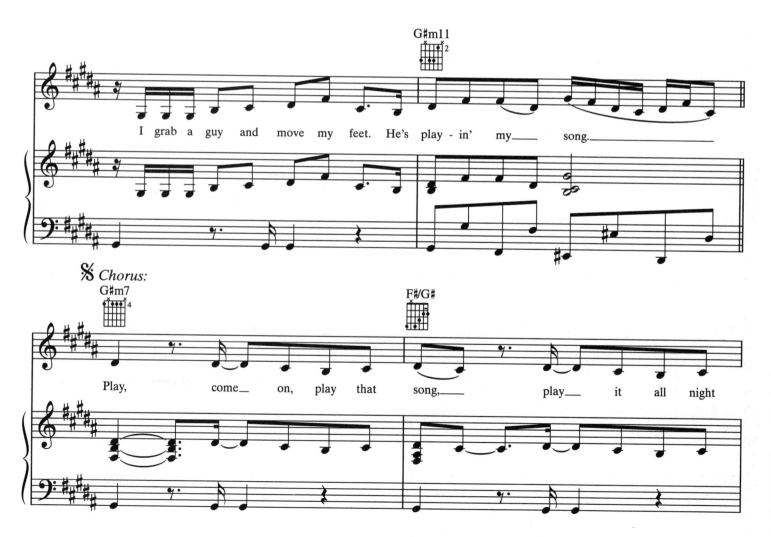

Play,   come___ on, play that   song,___   play___ it all night

long._____ Just turn it up__ and turn me on.

Play, come_ on, D. J. play that song,__ you know_ that it turns me

on. D. J., just play that song._ Just turn it up__ and turn me on.
'Cause I

D. J., just play that song,_ 'cause I wan-na be danc-in' all night long._ Well,

play my, play my, play my, play my,___ play my fav - 'rite song.

2.3.

G#m11

G#m7

wan - na be danc - ing all night long.___ Play, come___ on, play that

F#/G#

G#m7

song,___ play___ it all night long._____ Just

turn it up___ and turn me on. Play, come___ on, D. J. play that

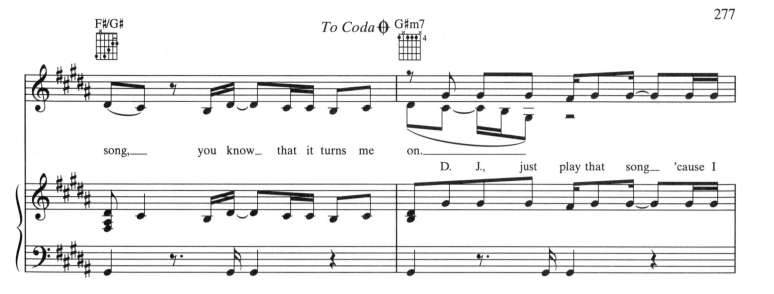

Chorus:

G#m7

Play, come__ on, play that song,__ play__ it all night long.__

Just turn it up__ and turn me on.

Play, come_ on, D. J. play that song,___ you know_ that it turns me

on.___ D. J., just play that song_ 'cause I wan-na be danc-ing all night long._

on.___ D. J., just play that song_ Just turn it up_ and turn me on.

Verse 2:
I don't care if everybody's gone,
Turn it up 'cause it turns me on.
Keep dancing all night long.
It feels so good that it can't be wrong.
I get the chills up and down my spine
Whenever I hear that song of mine.
When it stops, better press rewind.
Let me hear it one more time.
(To Chorus:)

POP

Words and Music by
JUSTIN TIMBERLAKE and
WADE J. ROBSON

Pop - 7 - 1

thing you've got to re - al - ize___ what we're do - in' is not___ a trend.

We got the gift of mel - o - dy,___ we're gon - na bring it 'til___ the end. Come on,___ now.___ (It does - n't

mat - ter___) 'bout the car I drive,___ what I wear a - round___ my neck.___ (All that

mat - ters___) Is that you re - cog - nize___ that it's just a - bout___ re - spect. (It does - n't

mat - ter___) 'bout the clothes I wear___ and where I go___ and why. (All that

mat - ters___) is that you get hype and we'll do it to you ev - 'ry - time.___ Come on___ now. Do you

Chorus:

ev - er won - der why this mu - sic gets___ you high? It

takes you on___ a ride. You feel it when your

body - y starts__ to rock and, ba - by, you__ can't stop. And the

1.

mu - sic's all__ you got. *This must__ be* Pop.

N.C.

Dirt - y Pop,__ ba - by, ba - by, you can't stop.__

I know you like this Dirt - y Pop.__ *This must__ be...* 2. Now,

Chorus:

Do you ev - er won - der why this

mu - sic gets___ you high? It takes you on___ a ride. You

feel it when your bod - y starts___ to rock and,

ba - by, you___ can't stop.   And the mu - sic's all___ you got.

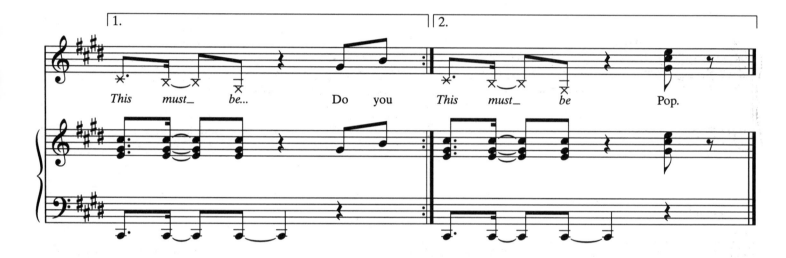

This must___ be...   Do you   This must___ be   Pop.

Verse 2:
Now, why you want to try to classify the type of thing we do?
'Cause we're just fine doin' what we like.
Can we say the same for you?
I'm tired of feelin' all around me animosity.
Just worry 'bout yours 'cause I'm-a get mine now.
People, can't you see...
It doesn't matter 'bout the car I drive or the ice around my neck.
All that matters is that you recognize that's it's just about respect.
It doesn't matter 'bout the clothes I wear and where I go and why.
All that matters is that you get hype and we'll do it to you everytime.
Come on.
(To Chorus:)

SIMPLE THINGS

Words and Music by
JIM BRICKMAN, DARRELL BROWN
and BETH NIELSEN CHAPMAN

Moderately ♩ = 92

(with pedal)

Verse:

1. Hey, time won't wait; life goes by.
2. So, here we go. Let's just dance;

Ev-'ry day's a brand new sky. Ev-'ry tear
teach my soul to take this chance. Put my heart

Simple Things - 5 - 1

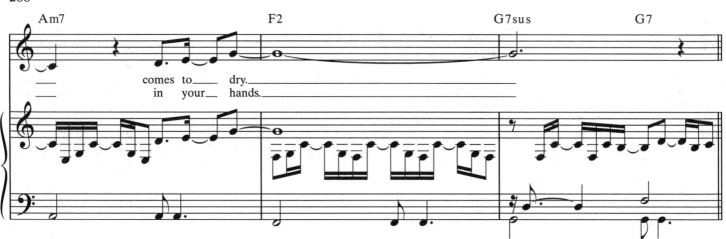

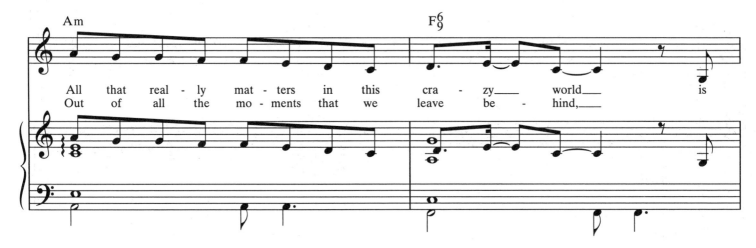

comes to___ dry._____
in your___ hands._____

All that real-ly mat-ters in this cra-zy___ world___ is
Out of all the mo-ments that we leave be-hind,___

you and I to-geth-er, ba-by. Just re-mem-ber:_____
turn a-round and tell me, ba-by; we'll re-mem-ber:_____

cresc.

℞ Chorus:

(1.) The first___ leaves off___ the tree;___ the way___ you look___ at
(2.) The thun-der and___ the rain;___ the way___ you say___ my
(3.) The o-cean and___ the sky;___ the way___ we feel___ to-

mf

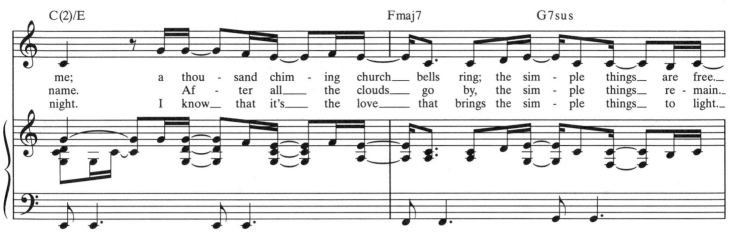

(I love the way_ the sim - ple things,_ the sim - ple things_ just____ are.)

Just____ are,

just____ are.

Repeat ad lib. and fade

SOMEONE TO CALL MY LOVER

Words and Music by
JANET JACKSON, JAMES HARRIS III,
TERRY LEWIS and DEWEY BUNNELL

Moderately fast ♩ = 128

Verse:

1. Back on the road a-gain. Feel-in' kind of lone-ly and look-ing for the right guy

spoil them when I'm in love, giv-in' them what they dream of. Some-times it's not a good thing,

Someone to Call My Lover - 5 - 1

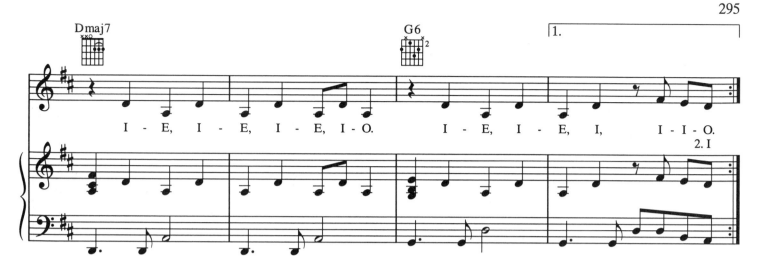

I - E, I - E, I - E, I - O. I - E, I - E, I, I - I - O.

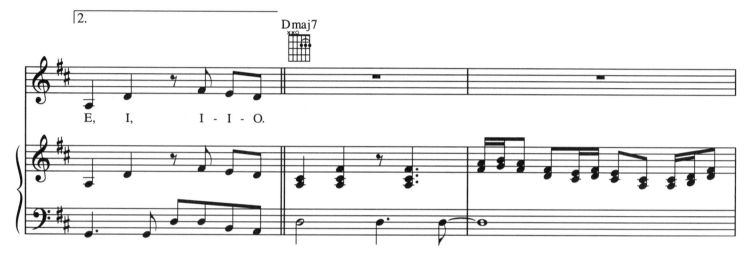

E, I, I - I - O.

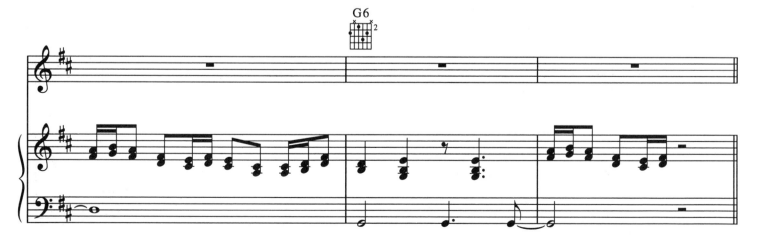

Bridge:

My, my, look-ing for a guy, guy. I don't want him too shy. But he's got-ta have the qual-i-ties that

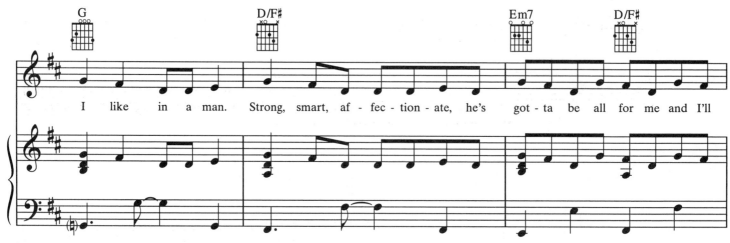

I like in a man. Strong, smart, af-fec-tion-ate, he's got-ta be all for me and I'll

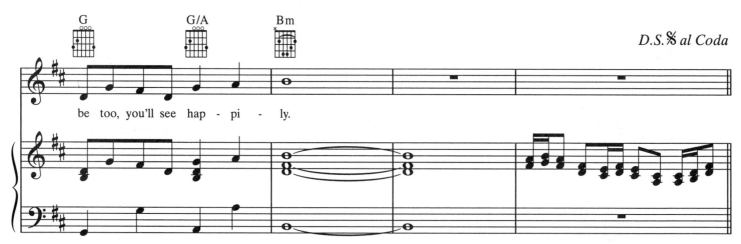

D.S. ℅ al Coda

be too, you'll see hap-pi-ly.

✠ *Coda*

get some-one to call my lov-er, yeah, ba-by, come on.

SOUTH SIDE

Words and Music by
RICHARD HALL

Moderato

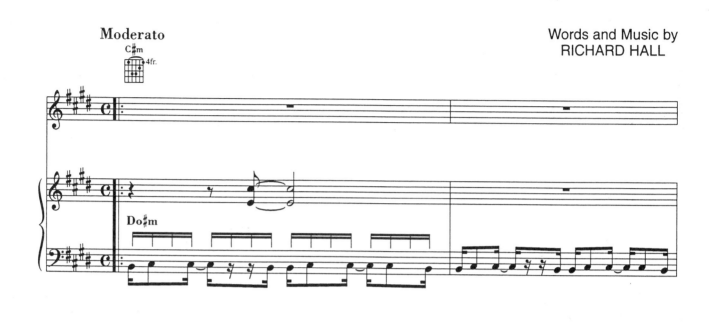

See my-self in the pour-ing home___
Here we are in the pour-ing home___

2nd times Guitar solo with the Voice

South Side - 5 - 1

see the light come o - ver now____
I watch the light man fall the comb____

see my - self in the pour-ing rain____
I watch a light move a - cross the screen____

I watch hope come o - ver me.____
I watch the light come o - ver me.____

Here we are____ now,____ going to the east side____ I pick up my____ friends____ and we
Here we are____ now,____ going to the west side____ wea-pons in____ hand,____ as we

SOON

Words and Music by
DIANE WARREN

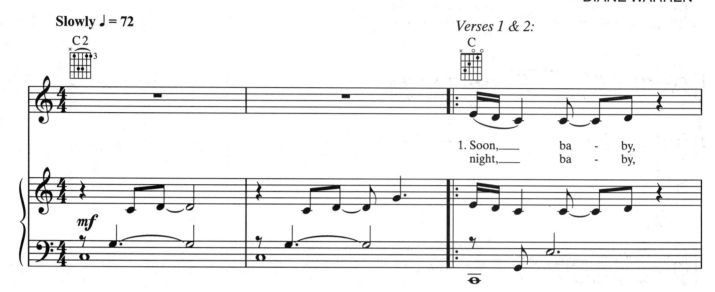

THE SPACE BETWEEN

Gtr. tuned down 1 whole step:
⑥ = D ③ = F
⑤ = G ② = A
④ = C ① = D

Words and Music by
GLEN BALLARD
and *DAVID JOHN MATTHEWS*

Chorus:

Repeat ad lib. and fade

Verse 2:
These fickle, fuddled words confuse me.
Like, will it rain today.
We waste the hours with talking, talking.
These twisted games we play.
(To Chorus 2:)

Chorus 4:
The space between the rain that falls,
Splashed in your heart,
Ran like sadness down the window into your room.
The space between our wicked lies is where we
Hope to keep safe from pain.

Chorus 5:
Take my hand, 'cause we're walking out of here.
Right out of here.
Love is all we need here.

Chorus 6:
The space between what's wrong and right
Is where you'll find me hiding, waiting for you.
The space between your heart and mine
Is the space we fill with time.

STANDING STILL

Words by
JEWEL KILCHER

Music by
JEWEL KILCHER and
RICK NOWELS

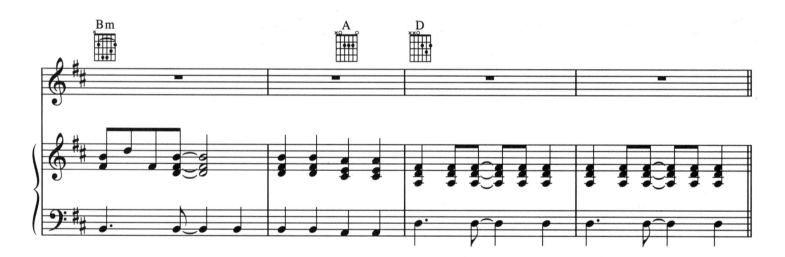

Verse:

1. Cut - ting through_ the_ dark - est night_ are my two head - lights._
2. *See additional lyrics*

Standing Still - 6 - 1

Try to keep it clear,__ but I'm los-ing it here__ to

the twi - light.___ There's a dead end to my left, there's a

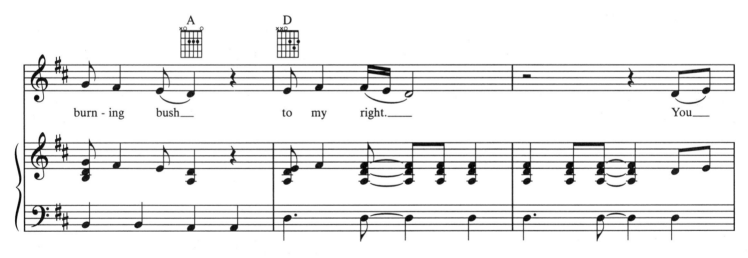

burn-ing bush__ to my right.___ You__

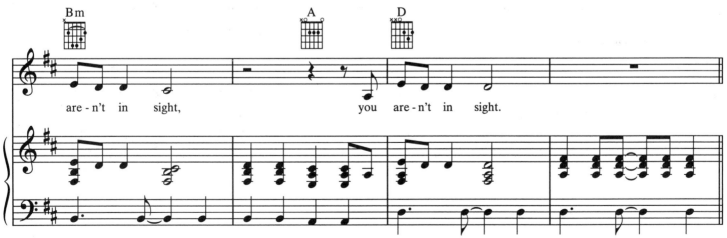

are - n't in sight, you are - n't in sight.

% *Chorus:*

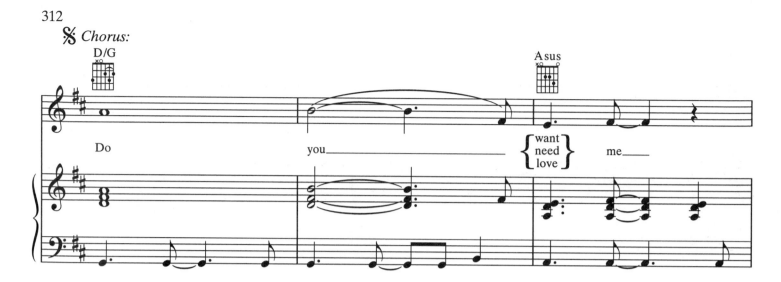

Do you { want / need / love } me

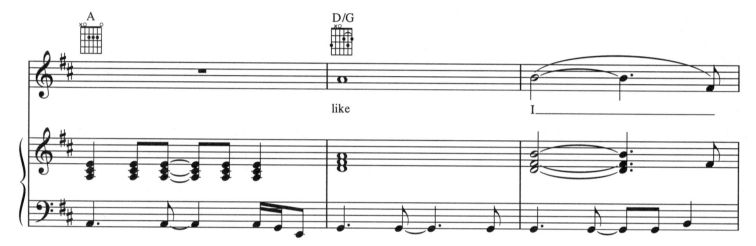

like I

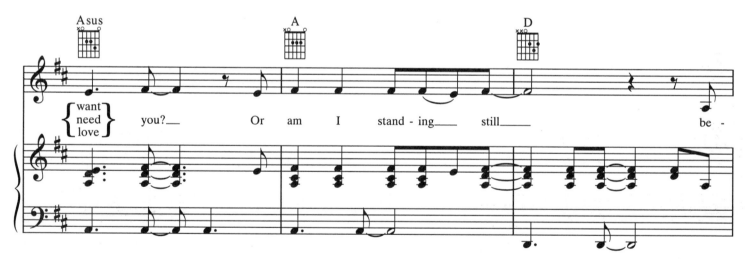

{ want / need / love } you?___ Or am I stand - ing___ still___ be -

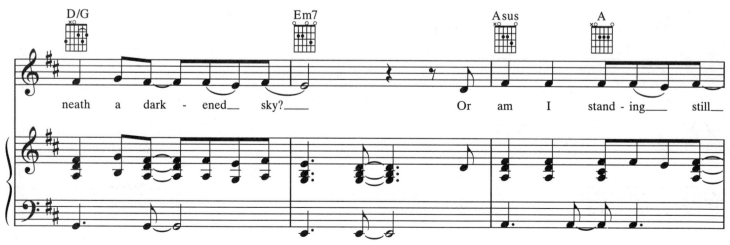

neath a dark - ened___ sky?___ Or am I stand - ing still___

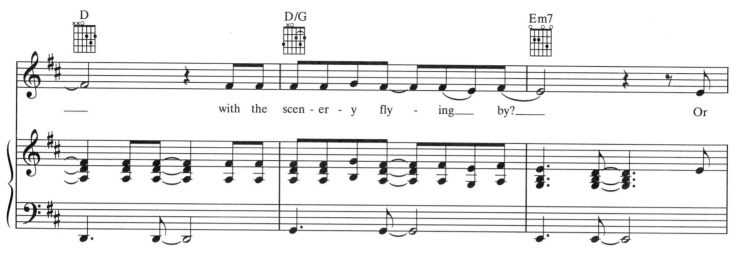

with the scen-er-y fly - ing___ by?___ Or

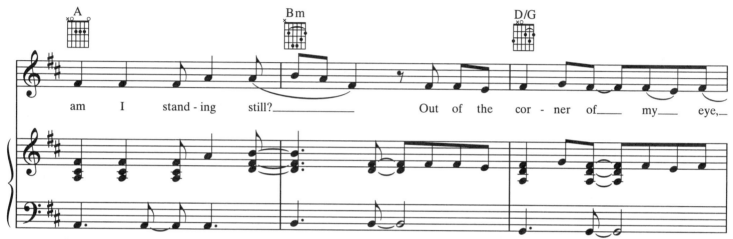

am I stand-ing still?_____ Out of the cor-ner of___ my___ eye,___

_____ was that you

To Coda

pass - ing me by?_____

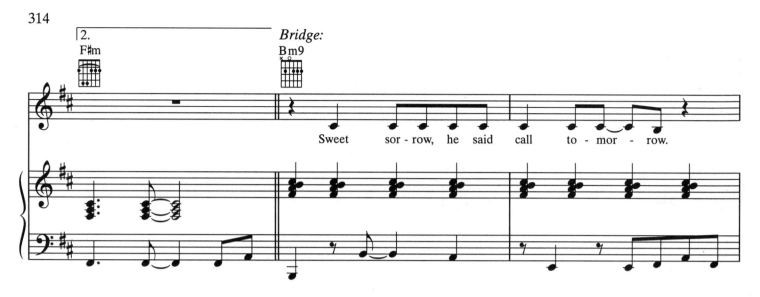

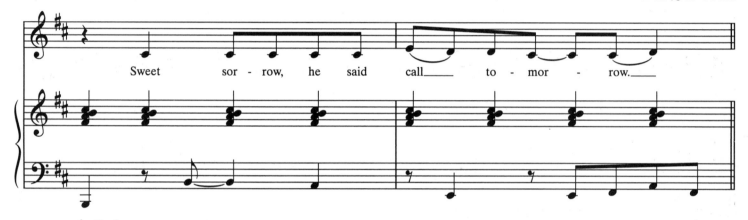

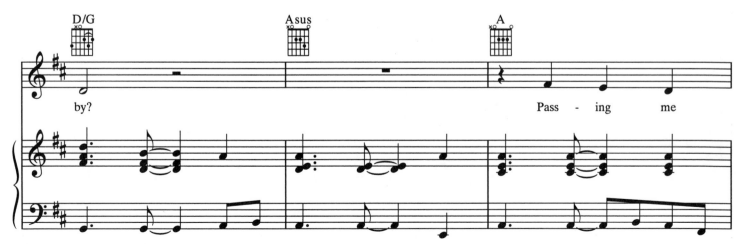

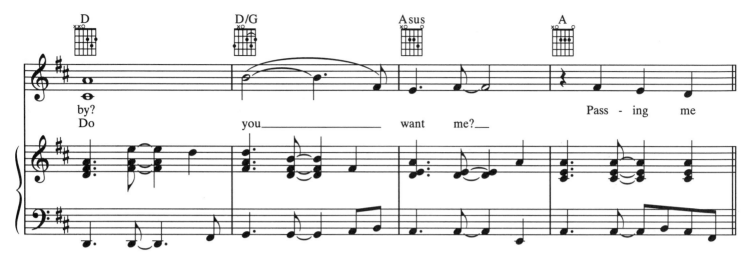

Verse 2:
Mothers on the stoop,
Boys in souped-up coupes
On this hot summer night.
Between fight and flight
Is the blind man's sight
And a choice that's right.
I roll the window down,
Feel like I'm gonna drown
In this strange town.
Feel broken down,
Feel broken down.
(To Chorus:)

SPANISH GUITAR

Words and Music by
DIANE WARREN

Slowly ♩ = 62

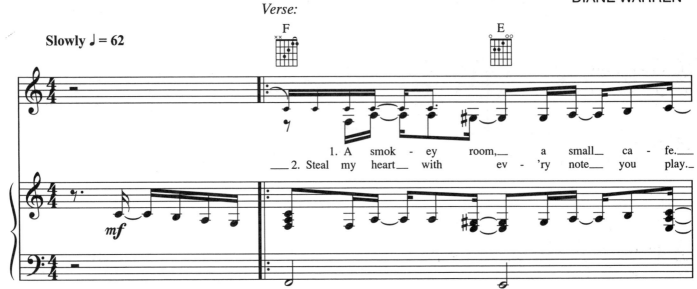

Verse:

1. A smok - ey room, a small ca - fe.
____ 2. Steal my heart with ev - 'ry note you play.

mf

They come to hear____ you play and drink and dance____ the night
I pray you'll look____ my way and hold me to____ your heart____

____ a - way.____
____ some - day.____

1.3. I sit____ out in the crowd____ and
2. I long____ to be the one____ that

Spanish Guitar - 5 - 1

close my eyes,___ dream you're mine.___ But you don't know,___ you don't e - ven know___ that
you car - ess____ with ten - der - ness.___ (3.) And you don't know,___ you don't e - ven know___ that

Chorus:

I am there._____ } I wish__ that I was in___ your arms___ like___ that
I ex - ist._____

Span - ish___ gui - tar, and you___ would play me through_ the night__ 'til__ the dawn.__

To Coda

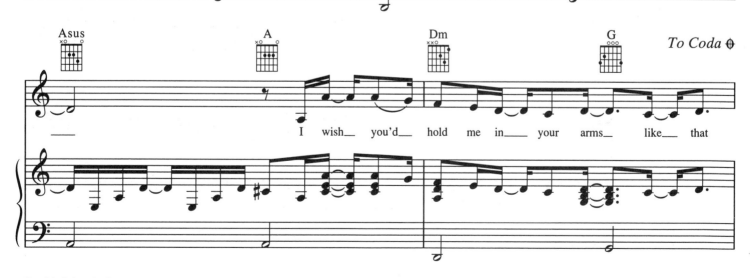

I wish__ you'd__ hold me in___ your arms__ like___ that

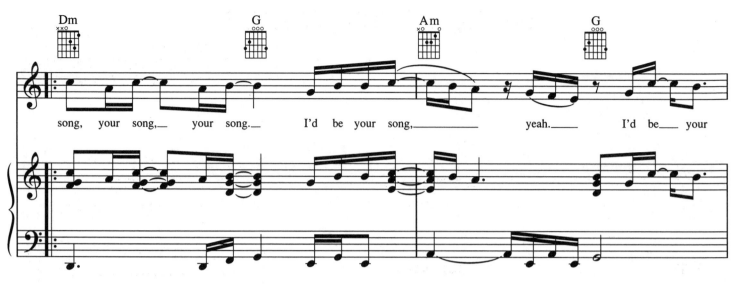

song, your song,___ your song.___ I'd be your song,_____ yeah.____ I'd be___ your

Repeat ad lib. and fade

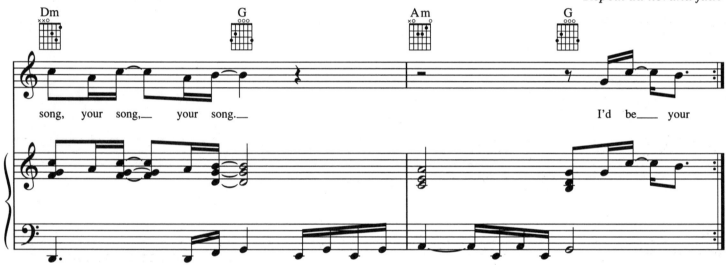

song, your song,___ your song.___ I'd be___ your

STILL ON YOUR SIDE

Words and Music by
DILLON O'BRIAN, BOB THIELE, JR., BRIDGET BENENATE,
MARK BARRY, CHRISTIAN BURNS and STEVEN MCNALLY

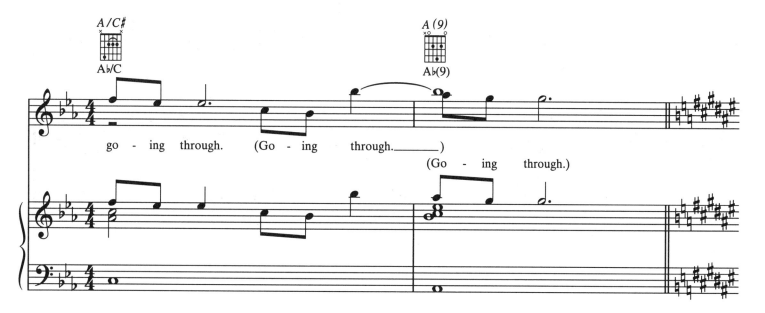

Still On Your Side - 5 - 1

324

Still On Your Side - 5 - 4

Chorus:

THE STORM IS OVER NOW

Words and Music by
R. KELLY

Slowly ♩ = 78

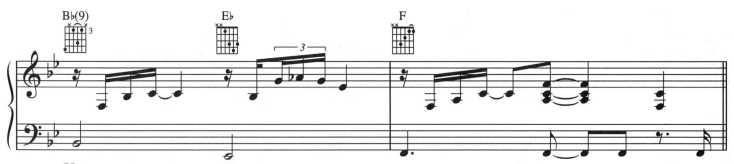

Verse:

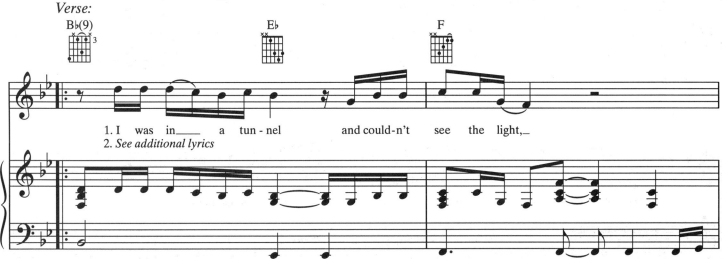

1. I was in___ a tun-nel and could-n't see the light,___
2. *See additional lyrics*

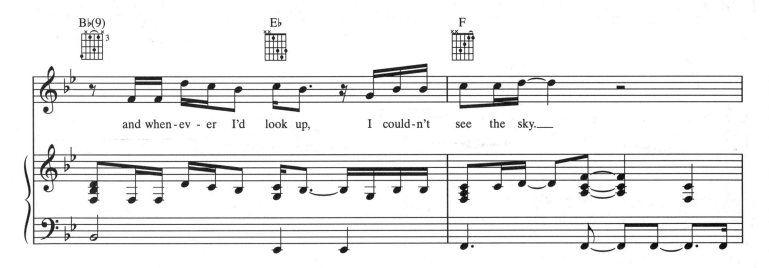

and when-ev-er I'd look up, I could-n't see the sky.___

The Storm Is Over Now - 7 - 1

Look like I_____ can see the light shin - ing down, down on me.

Look like I_____ can see the light shin - in'.

Repeat ad lib. and fade

Look like I_____ can see the light shin - in'.

Verse 2:
Now in the midst of my battle,
All hope was gone.
Downtown in a rushed crowd,
And I felt all alone.
And every now and then
I felt like I would lose my mind.
I've been racin' for years and still no finish line.
(To Pre-chorus:)

From Touchstone Pictures' PEARL HARBOR

THERE YOU'LL BE

Words and Music by
DIANE WARREN

There You'll Be - 5 - 1

THANK YOU

Words and Music by
DIDO ARMSTRONG
and PAUL HERMAN

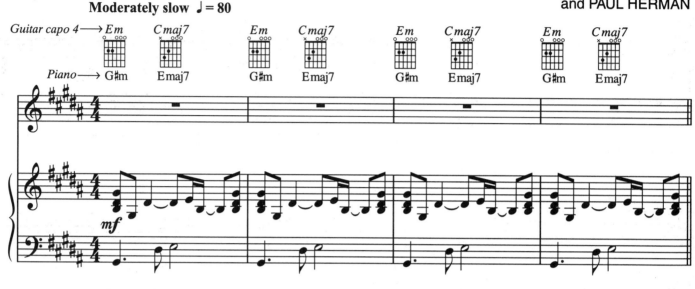

Verses 1 & 2:

1. My tea's gone cold, I'm won-d'ring why I got out of bed at all.
2. *See additional lyrics*

The morn-ing rain clouds up my win-dow and I can't see at all.

Thank You - 4 - 1

Verse 2:
I drank too much last night, got bills to pay,
My head just feels in pain.
I missed the bus and there'll be hell today,
I'm late for work again.
And even if I'm there, they'll all imply
That I might not last the day.
And then you call me and it's not so bad, it's not so bad.
(To Chorus:)

THIS IS ME

Words and Music by
PAM SHEYNE, DAVID FRANK
and STEPHEN KIPNER

This Is Me - 5 - 1

Verses 2 & 3:

2. Ba - by, I would nev - er do____ that.____ I love you faith - ful - ly.____

3. *See additional lyrics*

But, your sus - pi - cious mind thinks I'm gon - na re - peat her sto - ry.____ It's

mak - in' you cra - zy, mak - in' you a wreck, mak - in' you fol - low me, mak - in' me a sus - pect.

You seem to think I'm play - in' a game. Don't you know my name?____ That was her;

Chorus:

this is me. We're dif-fer-ent as can be. She and I are

noth-ing a - like. You're con-fus - ing day with night. That was then;

this is now. You wan-na trust me but you don't know how.____ I'm nev-er gon-na

mess a-round, let you down. Can't you see? That was her, and ba-by, this is me.

Verse 3:
Stop makin' me feel bad.
I'm the best thing you ever had.
Only thing I'm guilty of
Is givin' you too much love.
It's makin' you crazy,
Makin' you a wreck,
Makin' you follow me,
Makin' me a suspect.
You seem to think I'm playin' a game.
Don't you know my name?
(To Chorus:)

TOO LITTLE TOO LATE

Moderately fast ♩ = 144

Words and Music by
STEVEN PAGE and ED ROBERTSON

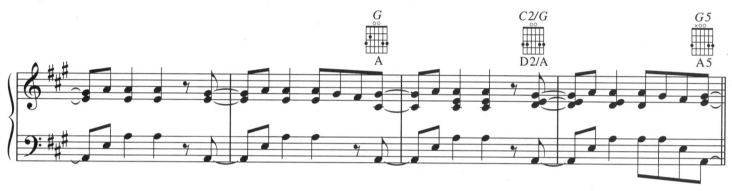

Verse 1:

1. You say, "Why does ev - 'ry - thing__ re - volve__

__ a - round__ you?"__ You say, "Why does ev -

Too Little Too Late - 7 - 1

Too Little Too Late - 7 - 5

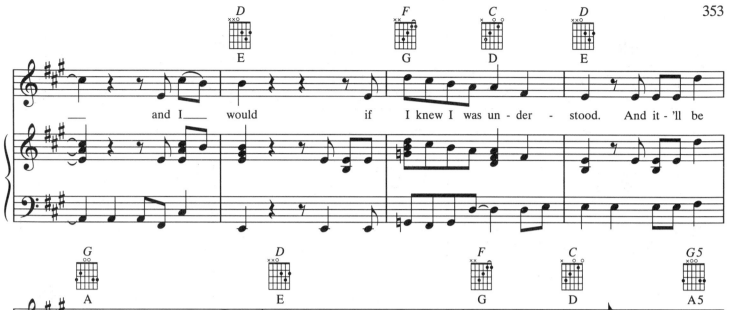

and I____ would   if I knew I was un - der - stood. And it - 'll be

great,   just____ wait,   or is it   too lit - tle too____ late?

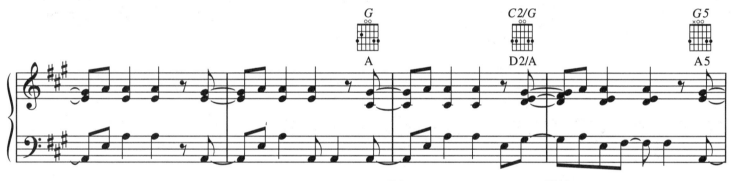

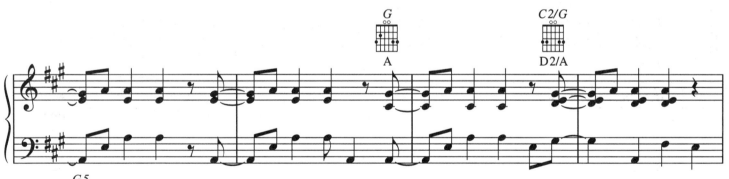

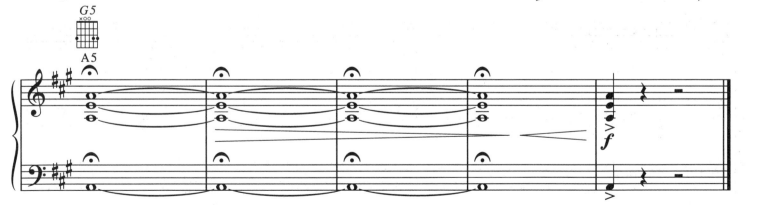

TURN OFF THE LIGHT

Words and Music by
NELLY FURTADO

Chorus:

U REMIND ME

Words and Music by
EDDIE HUSTLE
and USHER

U Remind Me - 4 - 1

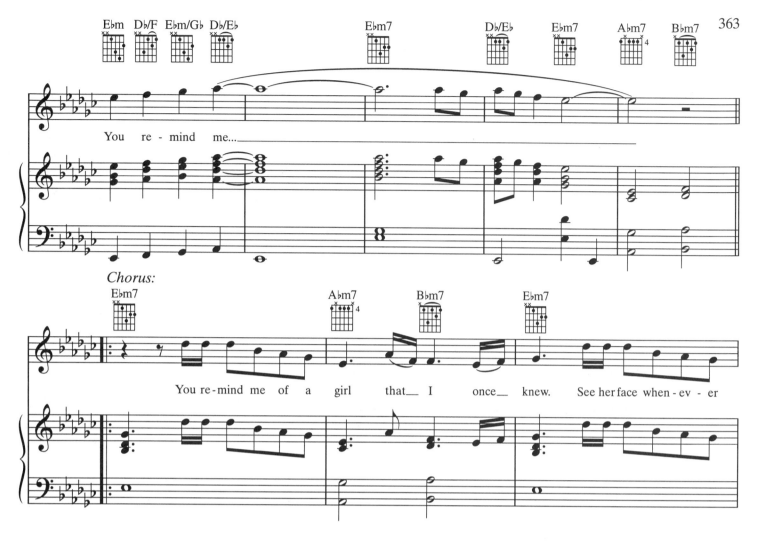

Chorus:

You re-mind me of a girl that__ I once__ knew. See her face when-ev - er

I, I look at you. You won't be-lieve all of the things she put me__

through.__ This__ is why__ I just can't get__with you.__ __ I just can't get__with you.__

WHAT IT FEELS LIKE FOR A GIRL

Words and Music by
MADONNA CICCONE
and GUY SIGSWORTH

Moderately ♩ = 104

What It Feels Like for a Girl - 6 - 4

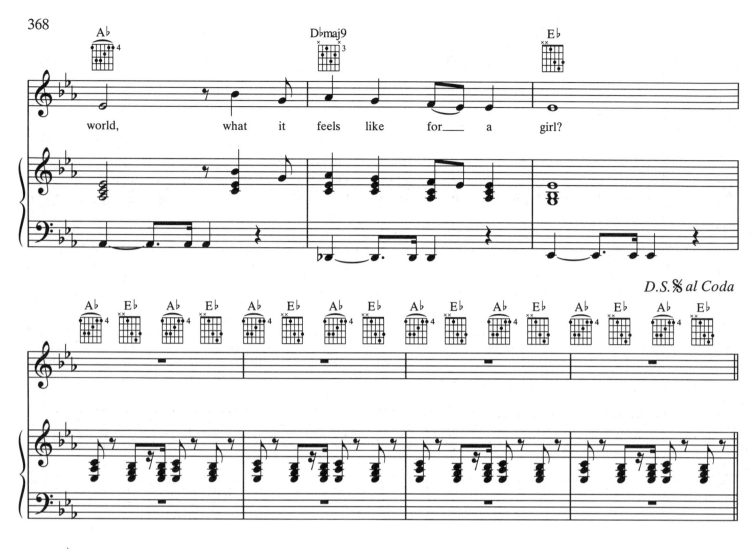

world, what it feels like for___ a girl?

D.S. 𝄋 al Coda

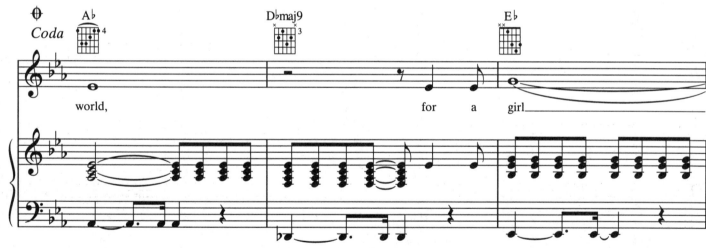

Coda

world, for a girl___

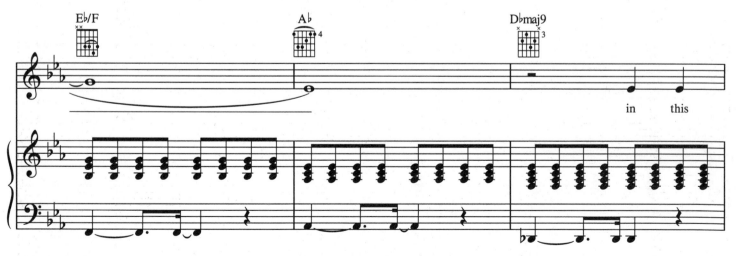

in this

WHEN IT'S OVER

Words and Music by
MARK McGRATH, STAN FRAZIER, RODNEY SHEPPARD,
CRAIG BULLOCK and MATTHEW KARGES

Moderately ♩ = 100

Verse 1:

1. When it's o - ver, that's the time_ I fall in love a - gain._

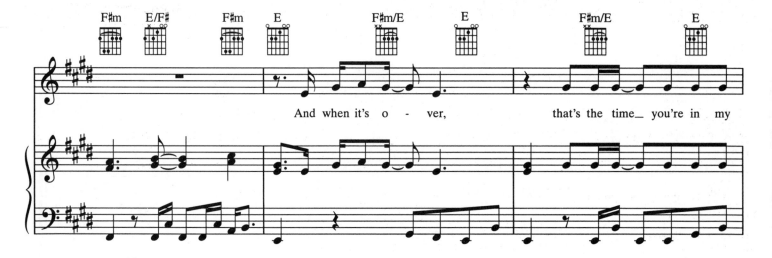

And when it's o - ver, that's the time_ you're in my

When It's Over - 6 - 1

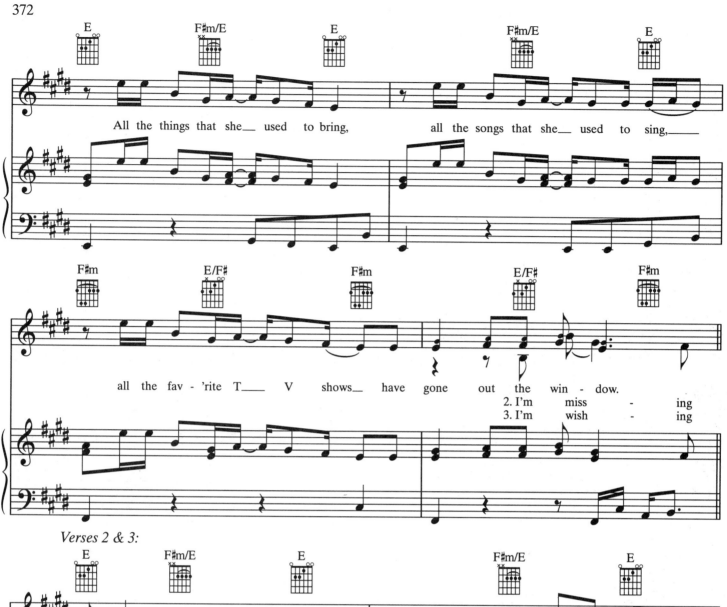

All the things that she__ used to bring, all the songs that she__ used to sing,__

all the fav-'rite T__ V shows__ have gone out the win-dow.

2. I'm miss - ing
3. I'm wish - ing

Verses 2 & 3:

you.__
you,__

I nev-er knew__ how much she loved__

__ me.
ing.

I'm miss - ing
I'm wish - ing

you nev-er said__ you were pre-tend -

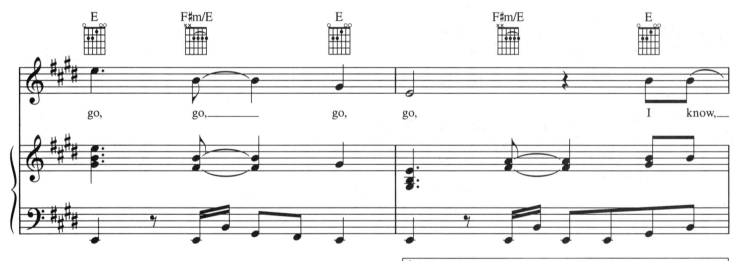

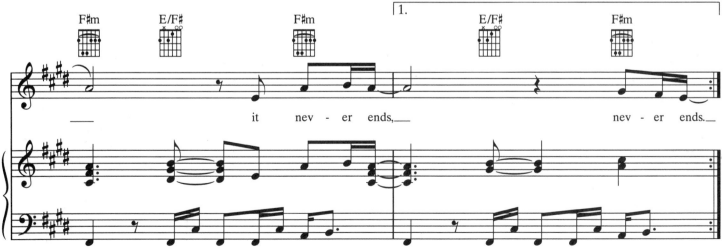

When It's Over - 6 - 4

Chorus:

All the things that I___ used to say, all the words that got___ in the way,___

all the things that I___ used to know have gone out the win-dow.

All the things that she__ used to bring, all the songs that she__ used to sing,___

Repeat ad lib. and fade

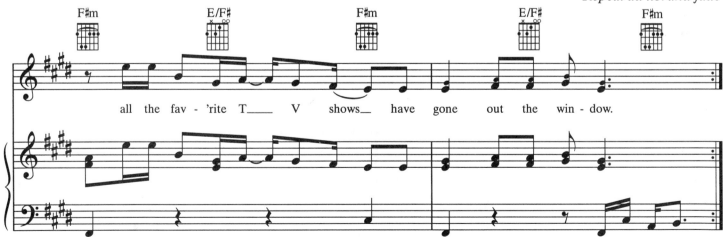

all the fav - 'rite T___ V shows__ have gone out the win - dow.

When It's Over - 6 - 6

WHENEVER, WHEREVER

Words by SHAKIRA
and GLORIA M. ESTEFAN
Music by SHAKIRA
and TIM MITCHELL

Moderately, freely ♩ = 92

Faster, with a dance beat ♩ = 112

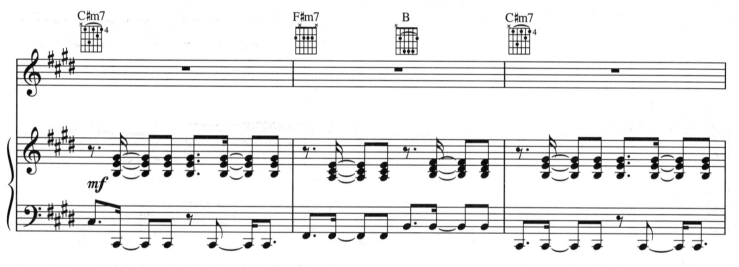

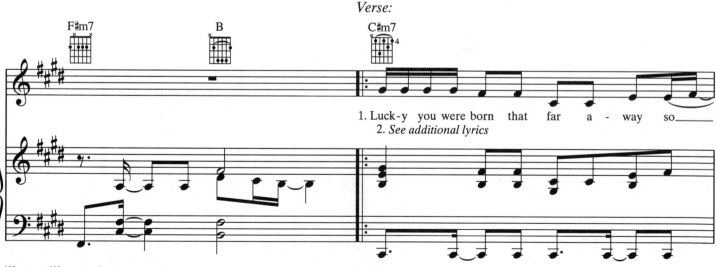

1. Luck-y you were born that far a-way so
2. *See additional lyrics*

Whenever, Wherever - 6 - 1

we could both make fun of dis - tance. Luck-y that I love a for-eign land for___

___ the luck-y fact of your ex - ist-ence. Ba - by, I would climb the An - des sole-ly___

___ to count the freck - les on your bod - y. Nev-er could i-mag-ine there were on-ly___

___ ten mil-lion ways to love some-bod-y. Le do lo le lo le,___

Chorus:

We can al - ways play by ear, but that's_ the deal, my dear.

Bridge:

Le do lo le lo le,_

le do lo lo lo le._____ Think out__ loud.__ Say it___ a - gain.___

Le do lo le lo le___ lo le.___ Tell me__ one__ more time_____ that you'll_ live___

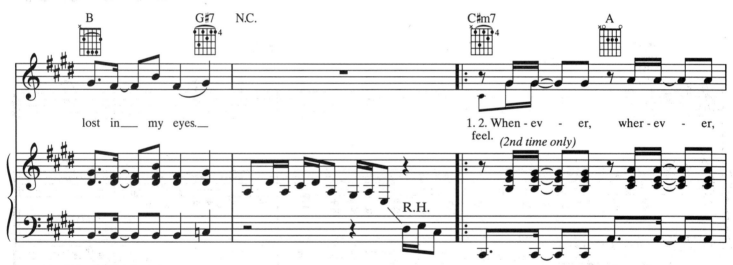

lost in__ my eyes.___ 1. 2. When - ev - er, wher - ev - er, feel. *(2nd time only)*

we're meant_ to be to - geth-er. I'll be there_ and you'll be near, and that's__ the deal, my dear.

There-o - ver, here-un - der; you've got___ me head o - ver heels.___ There's noth-ing left to fear

if you real-ly feel the way___ I___   if you real-ly feel the way___ I___ feel.

molto rit.   *freely*

Verse 2:
Lucky that my lips not only mumble,
They spill kisses like a fountain.
Lucky that my breasts are small and humble,
So you don't confuse them with mountains.
Lucky I have strong legs like my mother
To run for cover when I need it.
And these two eyes that for no other
The day you leave will cry a river.
(To Chorus:)

YOU CAN'T WALK AWAY FROM LOVE
(Music from the Motion Picture "ORIGINAL SIN")

Words and Music by
GLORIA ESTEFAN and
EMILIO ESTEFAN, JR.

388